To Mary,
and to seekers everywhere,
May the voice of your Spirit lead you home
to your own whole and holy Self.

My message is simply this:

"You are Good,
You are Beautiful,
You are Holy.
Step onto the path of your dream."

~ Kim Colella

CONTENTS

♡ *Listen* 53

🌿 *Manifest*

It is time to let go
of all that holds you back
from radiating your brilliance
into the world.

Vigeland Sculpture Park
Oslo, Norway, 2010

The Path to Spirit Embraced

I AM A SEEKER. FOR OVER thirty years, I have sought mentors, programs, experiences, and therapies to help me shift from a paradigm of fear, unworthiness, and shame to a paradigm of love, compassion, and truth.

My desire to grow has fueled the discipline of saying "Yes" over and over again to my spirit's urging to engage in pastoral therapy, movement therapy, body and energy work, yoga, women's groups, books, classes, and mentorships.

Spirit Embraced is about the extraordinary adventure that unfolded as I trusted and followed the voice of my spirit to release the trauma of my childhood, to follow my soul's urging to journey to Calcutta to spend time with Mother Teresa and the Calcutta L'Arche community, to manifest my deepest dreams and to tend the beautiful life I have created.

Spirit Embraced includes the tools I have used and continue to use, to grow into the most authentic and free version of myself and to help others to do the same. The tools I will describe are just that, tools. No one practice was *the* answer, but together these healing exercises have helped me transform old mindsets that no longer support my growth or relationships. I offer them to you to help support your journey.

Spirit Embraced contains four sections:

    Release

    Listen

    Manifest

    Tend

Each chapter in each section will have three parts:

    a story from my life,

    a tool of transformation that I have used to help me shift the paradigm of my life, and

    a soul psalm, a piece of writing from my journals that arose from listening to and embracing my spirit.

In each section, you will find murmurings of the qualities of the other sections. The process of transforming our lives is not linear, rather it is a circular process with each of these disciplines fueling the others. For instance, as I was writing the chapters for Manifest, I was surprised to discover that the foundation of this section was a story of loss. I found this curious. My intention was to write about birthing our dreams. As I reflected on this, I became aware that as we let go, if we choose to step forward, we enter this new space where magic can happen. We cannot enter into this space while we are holding on. It is when we feel naked and vulnerable, when we have let go, but have yet to fill the space, that we can receive.

Last fall, my son left for college. He chose a college in the Midwest, far from our home in the Pacific Northwest. During his junior year of high school, as we were busy touring colleges, I began the process of exploring how I would fill the space that his leaving home would create in me. I released my primary identity as full-time mother and welcomed the emerging role as mom of a young adult. Doing that, space in me began to open up. I didn't rush to fill that space. I took the time to listen, to imagine, to stand at the edge and to see what was beyond this familiar place of mom.

In that expanded space, with persistence and clarity, the voice of my spirit said, "Write."

I said, "What?!!!"

"Write. Tell the stories that long to be told."

In all honesty, I was terrified. And yet the voice continued to nudge and guide me. This book is the manifestation that came from stepping into that unknown.

I have had a blessed life, and this book is my legacy work. I have been given many experiences and angels in earth's clothing to call me forward. I offer you these stories and tools in the hope that in them you will find a remembrance of your own hidden wisdom to assist you on your own journey.

Blessings,
Kim

Release

It is time to let go of all that holds you back from
radiating your brilliance into the world.
It is time to surrender all the old habits and mindsets
that have constricted you
And made you smaller than who you really are.
As you release all that does not support your growth and healing,
space will open up,
allowing you to stretch towards
your most authentic and free self.

The Dance of Letting Go

It is a dance,

This letting go

Releasing the old voices of limitation

To welcome my true and

Limitless self

Home.

Gentle goodbyes to all that has held me in,

Clear the pathway to

Joyfully welcome

My prodigal self

Home.

Stop sneaking in.
Ask for what you want honestly and
Give me my choice again.

Vigeland Sculpture Park
Oslo, Norway, 2010

Nightmares

M Y EARLIEST CHILDHOOD MEMORY IS HIDING in the closet with my brothers and sisters in the dark of night. We sat in a row as if we were playing choo-choo train, praying the Our Father and Hail Mary over and over. I was two years old.

Earlier, Mom had called from our family grocery store. She anxiously told Joel, my thirteen-year-old brother, to gather up all of us kids and come to the store. Our dad was drunk and was on his way home. Joel and my older brothers and sisters, rushed to turn off the lights and get us out of the house before my dad arrived.

Just as the last light went off, Joel saw my dad's car come down the street. Twelve-year-old Jill ran to lock the doors. Seconds after she locked the back door, the knob jiggled as Dad tried to get in. As we tip-toed up the stairs in the dark to the second floor, my five-year-old brother, Rick, cried, "I want my daddy! I want to see my daddy!" My older brothers and sisters quieted him as they herded us into the closet.

As we prayed, we heard a crash from the basement. Dad was breaking in through a basement window. Our prayers became whispers as we heard him searching the first floor of the house. We heard him opening doors and closing them, calling out for us. We heard him come closer and closer…and then the footsteps stopped. He had passed out on the couch.

Mom arrived moments later. Hearing her mama bear energy call to us, we came out of our hiding space and quietly rushed to meet her in the dining room. She hurried us out of the house and into the family station wagon. Mom drove us around and around a nearby lake that night. When we returned home, a few hours later, Daddy was gone.

I am the seventh of eight children. We were all raised in a three-bedroom, one-bathroom house on the East Side of St. Paul, Minnesota, in a largely blue-collar neighborhood. There is a twenty-four-year difference between the oldest and the youngest child. The first five are quite close in age. The last three of us squeaked in at our leisure, creating our own unit. Someone once told me that every time my parents separated and reconciled, a pregnancy was the result. I see the three of us as the reconciliation babies.

By the time I was born in 1960, my dad was in late-stage alcoholism, and was in and out of our lives. I have worked to reclaim positive memories of my dad from my early childhood. As a small child, when I wore my red stretchy jumpsuit, Dad would throw me up in the air calling me his little red pepper as I squealed with glee. When my best friend and I were headed to a Saturday afternoon matinée, my dad put together a bag of penny candy for each of us. When I was five, Dad allowed me to use his cigarette rolling machine to roll his cigarettes for him. I loved the smell of the tobacco, the precision of laying the paper down just right and being entrusted with this adult task. These are the fatherhood treasures I carry.

For much of my life, however, the louder and more intrusive memories were the memories of him breaking in, of yelling and his violence.

When I was five, my eighteen-year-old sister Nancie and her fiancé took me to the circus. I adored Nancie and this evening of circus acts and cotton candy only made me love her more. Later that night, as I lay sleeping, Nancie and our sister Jill lay in their bed talking, Nancie was drinking a bottle of Diet Rite soda. My dad came home and when he saw that bottle of soda in their room, he went into a rage. He demanded to know whose it was. Timidly, Jill responded, "Nancie's." Dad picked up that glass soda bottle and hit Nancie in the face with it.

I awoke in the morning to a house in crisis. Nancie's face was bruised and swollen. I was so confused. How could Dad hurt my beloved Nancie? She was kind to everyone. She never got into trouble. She snuck me out of the house and took me to work with her if she felt one of my other siblings was going to hurt or bully me while she was gone.

Daddy sat me on his lap, told me to be a good girl, hugged me and said goodbye. When I asked where he was going, he replied, "I am going to see the priest." It would be three years before I saw him again. My mom had kicked him out for the last time. Dad spent those three years living on the streets.

During his third year on the streets, my dad watched one of his close friends die of Delirium Tremens (DT), severe alcohol withdrawal that is accompanied by shaking and/or hallucinations. This was a wakeup call for my dad. He had had many DTs and he knew he would not live through another. That day he sought treatment and began his journey to recovery. His alcoholic nightmare was over.

My nightmares would continue for another forty years. My dad died in 1975, just five years after he stopped drinking. And although he never lived with us again, in those last years, we had a chance to build positive memories during days together at the zoo and our annual visits to the Minnesota State Fair. Through our visits, I discovered that my dad had a great sense of humor, liked to wear bright green socks, and made delicious fried rice. Even though my positive images of my dad multiplied in those final five years of his life, the image of a dark, violent male continued to haunt me. So much so, that throughout my high school years, I slept with a butcher knife under my pillow. More than a few times, I woke up in the night screaming, awakened from a terrifying dream.

I am sorry, little one.
You are safe here.
You are safe.

Vigeland Sculpture Park
Oslo, Norway, 2010

Dreamwork

IN 2006 I TRAVELLED TO MINNESOTA over Memorial Day weekend to honor my elders, both living and passed. My mom had died the previous September. I visited her grave and then my dad's. I visited my godmother who was living with dementia and spent time at the College of St. Benedict with the nuns who had impacted my life while I was a student there.

My first night at St. Ben's, I had a dream: There was a knock at the front door. I asked, "Who is it?" There was no answer. I asked again, no answer. Standing on my tip toes, I peeked out the small window high up on the door. Staring back at me was a man, big and husky, wearing funky colors like orange and green. Afraid, I yelled at him, "What do you want?" I screamed at him, "Go away!" I told my young son Sam, to find the phone and call the police. When I looked out the window, again, the man was gone. I raced around the house, frantically looking for the phone, frustrated with Sam for not having found it.

I ran to lock the back door. I fumbled with the lock but it would not catch. I was so afraid he would get to this door before I could get the lock to work. As I fumbled, I noticed a crack in the wood on the main body of the door and my fear increased. As I frantically tried to secure the door, he grabbed me from behind. He had already gotten in through the door and I didn't know!

I woke up from this dream afraid and unsettled. I grabbed my journal and decided to dialogue with this man who haunted my dreams. I let my words and his responses flow without editing.

Who are you,
Silent man at my door?
I fear you.
I am terrified by your very presence.
What is it you are here to do?
Why must you force your way in?
Why do you grab me from behind?

I am your father,
Knocking at your door.
I am silent in my hope that you will recognize me and
Open your door to let me in.
I sneak in where I can.
I grab your attention.

You must stop.
I will welcome you, only if
You speak your name
And name your intentions honestly.
Stop sneaking in.
Stop terrifying me.
Ask for what you want honestly and
Give me my choice again.
Do not frighten me with your trickery
Or violence.
Come humbly and I WILL welcome you.

Kim, when you were a child,
I frightened you so many times:
Breaking into the house and
Threatening your mother.

I was intimidating, violent, and abusive.
I traumatized you. I am sorry.
I come to you in my orange and green shirt
To say I am sorry, little one.
You are safe here. You are safe.
I am sorry.
Drink in your life
With the same abandon that I drank my liquor,
For the life you have created
Is intoxicating!
Drink it in!
Drink in your husband and son.
Drink in your faith,
Your community of friends
And your work.
Drink in your dreams.
You can make them happen.
You DO make them happen.
Don't let your fear paralyze you.
Do not get stuck on securing splintered doors.
Go. Go freely.
Go joyfully in the direction of your dream.
I love you,
Dad.

After this dialogue, things shifted inside me. The dreams of the scary large man stopped and my comfort in the dark increased. Most importantly, I was able to finally forgive my dad and the frightened little girl inside me settled into calm. She finally felt safe.

Exercise: Dialogue with Your Dreams

Writing to our loved ones who have died or to the strangers in our dreams can hold potent information for us. It is a simple process.

- Find a comfortable place to sit with your journal and pen. If possible, light a candle.

- Plant your feet firmly on the floor, or if you are lying in bed, bend your knees and plant your feet firmly on the bed so that you feel the support of the earth.

- Take a few deep breaths…slow, deep breaths that fill your stomach and your chest.

- As you breathe, remember that the Hebrew word for breath is *Ruah*. This is the same word for Spirit. As you breathe, breathe in the Spirit of God, the Spirit of peace, protection, and healing.

- Now take your pen and journal and begin to write freely, without editing or censoring yourself.

- Allow yourself to write and as you hear responses, allow those to flow freely as well.

- Write until this feels complete.

- Take a few more deep breaths.

- Read what you have written and take in any important messages or learnings.

- Take one more long, slow cleansing breath.

- Blow out the candle to close this time.

Reconciling with My Greatness

Reconciling with my greatness.
Receiving all that is good.
Strong,
Deserving,
Powerful,
Inspiring,
Compassionate,
Clear, and
Beautiful
About my Self.
No longer keeping her hidden in
the closet,
Freeing her to dance in the light of day,
Swirling, twirling in her goodness,
Gulping in the joy of freedom,
Singing the deep, sweet swells
Of her spirit
Alive.

*What I really needed
was to hear the words, "I love you"
spoken with tenderness.*

Vigeland Sculpture Park
Oslo, Norway, 2010

There's No Room

I WAS THE BABY OF THE family until I was six years old. Even before my mom gave birth to my little sister, Kari, I knew my relationship with her was forever changed. I remember trying to crawl into my mom's lap for a cuddle late in her pregnancy and my mom pushing me away saying, "There's no room."

"There's no room." That became a mantra in my young heart. There is no room for my excitement, for my energy, for my tenderness, for my silliness, for my joy. There is no room for my spirit. There's no room. My mom never said these things, but it is how I interpreted the chaos around me.

My mom was one month pregnant with my youngest sister when she kicked my dad out for the last time. Now, here she was in her early forties preparing to give birth to her eighth child. My oldest sister was already married. At home, my mom had four teenagers, a nine-year-old, a six-year-old, which was me, and a baby on the way. As an adult, I can sympathize with her feeling overwhelmed, but as a child, I felt unwanted and unloved and my relationship with my mom became tumultuous.

I desperately wanted to be loved by my mom. Although she did all she could for us kids, what I really needed was to hear the words, "I love you" spoken with tenderness. She was unable to say those words to me, no matter how hard I tried. I became a "good girl" in an attempt to make her proud of me. I did well in school. I bought the things she said she had always wanted. I was committed to my faith. I was her only child to graduate from college. I received awards, I travelled the world and made a wonderful life for myself, yet her approval eluded me.

No matter what I did, in her mind, there was always a better choice I could have made. In second grade, I had my first ballet recital. I felt beautiful and graceful in my little blue tutu and ballet slippers. I performed my pliés with my back straight and my knees bent perfectly over my toes, and as I raised myself up into a relevé, I felt my joy and pride rise with me. When the dance was over, I ran down to sit with Mom in the second row. I was vibrating with excitement as I sat down. Before I had settled into my seat, the tap dancers took the stage. As they danced, my mom turned to me and said, "See? That's what you could be doing if you hadn't taken ballet." My little heart shriveled as all of my pride escaped like air leaving a pierced balloon.

When I was sixteen, my mom had a massive stroke. I had gone out with friends, thinking she had the flu. I got home just as the ambulance was pulling away to take her to the hospital. By the time I got to the hospital, my mom had become an old woman. Her hair and skin turned grey, the left side of her face drooped, and she was unconscious. For three days, she hung out at death's door. We did not know if she would stay with us or if she would let go into the comfort of death.

Slowly, she came back to us. She stayed in the hospital for months learning how to walk, cut her food, and get dressed — all with limited movement on her left side. Because I worked at this same hospital as a housekeeping aid, I was able to visit her every day. Each day I told her how much I loved her and needed her. Her only reply was, "OK, Honey" or "Ah-huh." After many weeks, I managed to sneak my younger sister, Kari, in to see her. (In those days, young children were not allowed in patient rooms.) As soon as Kari walked into the room, my mom put out her arms. Kari ran into them, and my mom pulled her to her chest and tenderly said the words I had longed to hear: "I love you, honey. I have missed you so much." My insides quaked with disappointment knowing that she was capable of saying those three words; she just could not say them to me.

In sixth grade, Father Cody came into my life and became my surrogate dad. For six years, he repeated to me, "Kimmer, there is more to life than the east side of St. Paul," and "Kimmer, you've got to go to college. You'll make a good nurse." When I was a senior in high school, "Cods" took me up to the College of St. Benedict, an all women's Catholic college about ninety minutes from the Twin Cities and told me that this is where I needed to go after high school. Father Cody made sure I had a tour of the campus and a meeting with the financial aid office. When I returned home that evening, my mom was standing at the stove making dinner. Eagerly, I told her that I wanted to go to college and I wanted to go to the College of St. Benedict. She stopped her stirring and with a look of confusion asked, "Where do you think we are going to get that money?" I told her I had met with the office of financial aid and I was going to pay for it with grants and loans. She said little more and went back to her stirring. What I had hoped for from her was excitement; what my spirit heard was an uninspired, "Good Luck."

These three stories of my relationship with my mom are samples of the pattern of our relationship. I share these stories because over time this pattern of how we related to each other developed in me feelings of self-doubt, unworthiness, distance, and isolation.

———————◆———————

My relationship with Mom began to heal when I was in my early twenties. I was working as the director of marketing and advertising at a local bank, and I was living in a house with three other young women. The distance gave each of us more breathing room. As I became more independent, my dependence on her approval lessened. During this time, a friend invited me to go on an intergenerational Catholic weekend retreat. I was so moved by the experience that I volunteered to work on the retreat for ten of the next twelve retreats offered. I encouraged Mom to participate in one such weekend. To my surprise, she agreed to go. What she did not know was that all weekend, I was there, too, working behind the scenes as part of the team cooking, cleaning and praying for those on retreat. Towards the end of the weekend, after a talk on loving service, they introduced the support team. When my mom saw me, she hugged me and said, "I love you, honey, and I always have." I felt my heart begin to heal.

Participating in this retreat program gave me the courage and clarity I needed to leave my job at the bank and join the Jesuit Volunteer Corps in the Pacific Northwest. In August of 1984, I moved across the country to Washington State. My intention was to do one year of service as a youth and elderly minister in Eastern Washington. That one year turned into two years of service. After the second year, I moved to Western Washington and made it my home.

In 1987, I began working with an incredible therapist who helped me unpack the unhealthy patterns of my childhood and shift the paradigm of my life. Four years into my therapy, my mom came for a visit, and I asked her to see my therapist with me. Again, to my amazement, she agreed. My therapist started by telling her that she was there as a consultant for me, that there were things I was trying to work out that I believed she had already lived through, and that I would like her input.

I asked my mom questions like,

"Mom, I feel abandoned by the men in my life. I imagine you must have felt abandoned by Dad. How did you get through it?"

She replied, "I just had to, for the children."

"Mom, I feel betrayed. Have you ever felt that way? How did you handle it?"

"I focused on the children."

With each response, I came to see that it was her love and commitment to her children that kept her going, even in her most difficult and painful moments. I came to see her deep love for her children and recognized that since I was one of her children, she must deeply love me. Another layer of our relationship was healed.

I married Niko in 1995 when I was thirty-five years old. At thirty-eight, I gave birth to our son, Sam. I was a little more than a year older than my mom was when she gave birth to me, her seventh child. Four years later, Niko's mom, Jerry, was diagnosed with inoperable cancer. Niko and I agreed that you only get to journey with someone to their death once, there is no "re-do" once they are gone. As her illness progressed, he took three months off work to support his mom in her dying. He spent three and a half days a week at his parent's home, on the other side of the mountains, and then came home for three and a half days to be with Sam and me. While he was home, he cooked dinners, did laundry, cleaned the bathroom and made sure I had some time to myself.

Two months into this routine, I called my mom and asked, "How did you ever do it?"

"How did I do what?" She asked.

"How did you raise eight kids on your own? How did you keep your sanity? I have one child, one sweet little boy. Niko is only gone three and a half days a week and when he comes home, he is fully present and helps out around the house. Yet, I'm losing my mind! I'm not made out to be a single parent. I am not strong enough. I don't know how you did it, Mom!"

On the other end of the phone, all I could hear was her giggle. Another layer healed. As a mother myself, I experienced only a fraction of the challenges that my mom faced. I felt deep compassion for the overwhelm she had experienced and grateful for all she gave me in the midst of it.

I feel elated in the celebration
Of my spirit revealed.
I know I am loved.

Vigeland Sculpture Park
Oslo, Norway, 2010

Rewrite the Painful Past

THE UNRESOLVED WOUNDS FROM OUR PAST keep us stuck. Even though I had spent years in counseling and had forgiven my mom for any ways she had hurt me, I still experienced residual self-doubt in making decisions and blocks within me to feeling lovable.

The following exercise was powerful for me. Five years ago, I did a mentorship with Jean Houston, who is considered the founder of the Humanistic Psychology Movement. During a three-day workshop in her home, she talked about the power of rewriting our past. I decided to take those three moments with my mom that had left a painful mark on my soul and rewrite them into the story I had hungered to live.

Mama, I dance for you.
I point and plié and twirl and dip.
Radiant in my first blue tutu,
I am a ballerina
And I am proud.
You watch me
And your face is filled with joy.
I run to you
And you celebrate my brilliance.
You clap your hands,

You laugh, you smile,
You stroke my face with wonder and delight.
I feel elated in
The celebration
Of my spirit revealed.
I know I am loved.

Mama, I come to you
As you lie in the hospital,
Dancing between worlds,
Deciding to stay or to go.
I beg you, Mama,
Please stay!
Stay here on earth as my mom.
I whisper my deep love of you over and over.
I beg you to stay here for me.
You open your eyes and
Radiate your deep love of me.
You promise to stay.
You stroke my hair and
Assure me of your deep love, and
Belief in me, your daughter.
I feel safe.

Mama, I am bubbling with excitement!
I tell you of my dream to go to college.
I have made my choice.
I am going to the College of St. Benedict.
Your face lights up with joy.
You look deeply into my eyes.
Your deep blue pools reflect the depth of your pride.
You cheer me on.
You tell me to go for it, and
I believe in my dream.

The results were immediate and lasting. This exercise took the power out of the pain. Now when I think back on these experiences, there is no emotional charge. I can remember my mom with joy and gratitude. And I live with a greater sense of ease and freedom.

Exercise: Rewrite Your Painful Past

- Sit with your journal and pen in a quiet space.

- Identify key moments in your life that planted seeds of self-doubt or that hold you back in any way.

- Imagine how those moments could have unfolded in ways that would have strengthened your spirit.

- Rewrite the memory in detail as if it really happened in a way that fed, nurtured, and strengthened your spirit.

- Read this new memory you have created.

- Take note of how you feel when you read this new memory.

- Breathe it in.

Rewriting your old painful memories into the story your soul hungers to live can help you quiet the static of the inner messages that keep you from radiating your full brilliance into the world.

Song of the Great Mother

Lullaby my little one.
Lullaby, my sweet.
Rest your spirit
In my love.
Come home again to me.

I am lovable.
Just because I am
A creation of God.

Vigeland Sculpture Park
Oslo, Norway, 2010

You Are Worthy of Love

IWAS NINE YEARS OLD AND lying in bed one night when a feeling of deep love came over me. I felt God's love totally and completely for me, in me, and through me. I said a deep "Yes" that night to living a life committed to serving that love.

It was confusing to me how I could feel such a deep and abiding love from God and yet still feel unlovable. It is not as if my family life changed overnight. There was still pain and arguments and yelling. I still needed to read a room quickly to know if I was safe or in trouble. I had a sister who told me often that I was so ugly or stupid that I stunk. And I had a brother going through puberty that liked to use me as his punching bag. The paradigm of "power over" was alive and well in our household, yet at nine years old, I somehow knew that I would and could have a different life for myself.

That moment, when I felt the deep love come over me, was when my spiritual journey began. It was a slow journey. As long as I lived in my family home, fear walked with me. Yet, from the moment I made my commitment to love, in the dark of that night, I began to seek out and attach myself to people who affirmed my goodness and modeled for me a different way to live.

There have been countless people, my angels in earth's clothing, who have called me home to myself. One such person was Ben. Ben was my boss when I was a youth minister in my mid-twenties. He gave me two gifts: one that forever changed my experience of conflict and the second challenged my core beliefs about myself.

Working in ministry can be all-consuming. No matter how many days and hours I worked, there was still more to be done. I made a commitment to myself that from the time I left church after Mass on Sunday until Tuesday morning it was "Kim time," and I would not do any work or go to the church for any reason. After a few weeks of this new schedule, Ben began to needle me about it, saying things like, "It sure must be nice to have so much time off." I grew angry and defensive. Didn't he see how much I worked? Didn't he recognize how much time and energy I gave to these kids?

With my insides quaking, I went to talk to Ben. I had proof that I was working more than my forty-hour commitment and records proving that I was fulfilling all the items on my contract. I had all the ammunition I would need for the battle ahead.

Ben immediately disarmed me. As I sat down, I asked Ben if he was dissatisfied with my work or if he felt I was neglecting my duties. He looked at me with confusion and asked me why I would ask him that question. I recounted the many remarks he had made about my commitment to time off. He sat back in his chair and became very quiet. Then he looked up at me and told me he was so sorry. When he was my age, Ben was a Trappist monk. Life in the monastery was very structured; every minute of every day was scheduled for him. He realized through our discussion that he had been feeling a bit jealous of my freedom and he asked me to forgive him. Ben was the first person I had ever told that I was angry or hurt who did not dismiss my feelings or turn the tables and make it my fault.

My second experience with Ben occurred after I witnessed the birth of my godson, Wesley. The experience of seeing that precious baby come into the world was so beautiful and awe-inspiring! I had sixteen years of

Catholic schooling behind me and had heard my share about original sin. I could believe that I, Kim, came into the world imperfect or stained with sin but this beautiful being? No way! There was something seriously wrong with this teaching.

I marched into Ben's office to ask him—a great scripture scholar and one of the holiest people I knew—what he thought about the doctrine of original sin. His response is the only definition of original sin that makes sense to me.

"We come into the world in the perfect image and likeness of God, each and every one of us. Because we come into an imperfect world, with imperfect parents, teachers, school systems, churches, etc., original sin eventually enters all of our lives. It enters our lives the moment we are told and believe that we must earn our love. Then we forget that we are lovable just because we are a creation of God. We spend the rest of our lives trying to unlearn this untruth."

This description rang true in the deepest part of my being. I could see how hard I had been working to prove myself worthy. From that day forward, I shifted my focus to reclaiming within myself that I am lovable—because I am a creation of God.

You are Good.
You are Beautiful.
You are Holy.

Vigeland Sculpture Park
Oslo, Norway, 2010

A Mantra to Shift Outdated Beliefs

To help myself embody this new belief system that I was lovable just because I am a creation of God, I knew I would need strong medicine. The old lie was so loud in me that I created this powerful mantra for myself:

I am Good. I am Beautiful. I am Holy.

I am Good. I am Beautiful. I am Holy.

As I step out of bed in the morning, I whisper,

"I am Good. I am Beautiful. I am Holy."

With each step I take, I repeat:

"I am Good. I am Beautiful. I am Holy."

When fear threatens to stop me in my tracks, I remind myself:

"I am Good. I am Beautiful. I am Holy."

With each inhalation, I imagine this truth taking root in me.

As I exhale, I imagine myself radiating these qualities into the world.

I repeated this mantra over and over daily for many years until I believed it in every cell of my being. It is a mantra I continue to use whenever I feel anxious or have a difficult conversation ahead or whenever self-doubt creeps in.

As I infused my life with this mantra, it began to expand outward into the world.

Not only did I repeat, "I am Good. I am Beautiful. I am Holy."
But my prayer continued:

"You are Good. You are Beautiful. You are Holy."

As I approach a difficult situation or conversation:

"I am Good. I am Beautiful. I am Holy."

And as I look upon the face of the others involved, I whisper in my heart:

"You are Good. You are Beautiful. You are Holy."

As I prepare to see a client, I ground myself in this truth: "I am Good. I am Beautiful. I am Holy."

As I meet with my client, I pray that through my presence their spirit hears, "You are Good. You are Beautiful. You are Holy."

As I stand in wonder, I hear, "I am Good. I am Beautiful. I am Holy."

And my soul sings, "This life, this world, it is Good. It is Beautiful. It is Holy."

As I grow in my ability to love myself unconditionally and completely, I am better able to radiate these qualities into the world and I can better reflect to others their incredible worth and beauty, just because they are an amazing creation of God.

Exercise: Create a Personal Mantra

- What is the most terrifying love song your soul wants to sing to you?

- What are the words you most long to hear, yet are afraid to believe about yourself?

- Dare now to say these words over and over to yourself for many days, months, years, until you believe them in every cell of your being.

- Create your mantra and reclaim your sacred birthright!

Sing in Me a New Song

Sing in me a new Song,
So beautiful and true,
That the old, slow tune
Of my past existence,
No longer resonates in
This new place of myself.

Breathe into me the
Story of my life's path
With such force that it
Takes my breath away
And I gulp…
I gulp in this new reality
Of ME,
Fully Lived.

*I assured her that I would always
Carry her in my heart,
And I said goodbye.*

Vigeland Sculpture Park
Oslo, Norway, 2010

Heart-Centered Goodbye

IN AUGUST OF 2005, I GOT the call. My mom had advanced colon cancer that had metastasized sixty percent of her liver. My family was reeling from the news and had little information. They did not know what we could expect next, or whether she had days, weeks or months to live. I called my friend, Steve, a physician who always answers my questions with honesty and clarity. Steve was clear. If I wanted to spend time with my mom before she died, I should go see her as soon as possible. She had about two weeks to live.

Relief swept over me. After Mom's massive stroke in 1976, we were told that she would not survive another major stroke. Her doctors warned us that she probably would not live another five years. I had spent my entire adult life expecting a call that Mom had had another major stroke and was either unconscious or dead. This call with Steve was different. I had two weeks! Two weeks to be with my mom, to say my goodbye and to journey with her, in this final stage of her life. What an incredible gift!

Only a few days before, I had called Mom to wish her a happy birthday and to tell her that I wished I could be there for her birthday party at my brother's cabin the next day. During our phone visit, I learned that she was not feeling well, again. For months, she had been having bouts of nausea that left her unable to eat. I was worried. When I exclaimed, "Mom, this is happening too frequently!" she assured me that she had been to the doctor. Her doctor had focused on her long history of cardiovascular disease and gave her nitroglycerin pills. Mom was sure it was just the flu.

That next day, my family gathered at my brother's lake cabin in Wisconsin to celebrate Mom's birthday. Late that evening, as Mom was getting ready for bed, she went to the kitchen to take her evening pills. My family heard what sounded like a bowling ball hitting the floor. They ran into the kitchen and found Mom lying on the floor. She had fallen off her chair, her glasses lay shattered, and her face was bleeding. Unable to get her up, they called for an ambulance and Mom was transported to a small, rural hospital where the doctors had no records of her health history and therefore, no preconceived notions about her health. After a full examination, the doctor determined that there were no major injuries from her fall, just two black eyes and a cut on her nose. He was, however, very concerned about her nausea and ordered tests on her gallbladder and liver. She had fallen on Saturday. By Tuesday, the test results were definitive. She had advanced colon cancer.

Two days later, I boarded a plane to Minnesota to go be with my mom and family. When I arrived at the hospital, six of my seven siblings were there, the television was on, and things were quite busy. Although I had hoped for some quiet one-on-one time with Mom, I knew that with my large family this busyness was to be expected. I prepared myself for little to no time alone with her. So, I was amazed and elated when everyone left by 7:00 p.m. and said they would be back at 10:00 the next morning. I felt like I had won the lottery.

I love the quiet of the night. Even in a hospital, things quiet down and there is much less activity, less poking and prodding. I find the nighttime to be the most precious time to sit with someone. As life quiets down, the opportunities for intimate conversation expands.

Each night while I was there, I had the honor of sitting at Mom's bedside. For the first two days and nights, she was so heavily medicated that she was not coherent and mostly was asleep. On Sunday, they changed her meds. Late that night, Mom woke up.

She looked at me with clarity and asked, "When are they going to do my surgery?"

I took a deep breath and with all the love and tenderness I had, I said, "They are not going to do surgery, Mom. The cancer is too advanced, and there is a high probability that you would not survive surgery."

"What are they going to do?" She asked.

"They are just going to let things take their course, Mom. As soon as your apartment is ready, we will take you home. They are delivering a hospital bed and equipment that will be needed to care for you there. A hospice nurse will be available to give you medications to keep you comfortable. We will all be with you, and we will drink in every moment we have with you."

Mom got very quiet. Then she turned her back to me, curled into herself and spent the next few days cocooned in sleep.

On Monday, Mom was officially put on hospice and sent home. I continued to spend my nights resting next to her bed and catching any moments I could with her. When she was awake, she answered questions in one- or two-word sentences and seemed very guarded towards me. My prayer, during this time, was that she would open up and be able to receive my love for her before I had to leave early Wednesday morning.

Wednesday morning at 1:00 a.m., my prayers were answered. Mom woke up, grabbed my hand, and looked at me with deep love. All I could say was, "Thank you." We sat together for the next three hours, and I said everything I longed to say to her. I asked for her forgiveness. I expressed my deep love for her. I told her I would be OK. I assured her that I would always carry her in my heart. And I said goodbye. Her responses were loving and tender. I felt loved, seen and embraced by my mother, and decades of pain were healed.

At 4:00 a.m., I left St. Paul to return to my home in Tacoma, Washington. My intention was to see clients for a few days and then return to Minnesota the following Wednesday and to stay as long as was needed. When I returned home from work that afternoon, I called to check on Mom. The hospice nurse told me that my mom had taken a turn for the worse and was not expected to live through the weekend. She encouraged me to return as soon as possible. I jumped into the task of finding child care for Sam. Niko had just started a hospice residency and could not take time off. As I was struggling to get all of Sam's coverage taken care of, Sam came up to me and said, "If I don't get to see Grandma Jane before she dies, I am going to be so mad, Mom." I took a deep breath, shifted the course, called my best friend in Minnesota and asked if she and her family would host Sam for a couple of days. With her immediate yes, I packed up the two of us and was on a plane, just thirty-six hours after I'd returned home.

When Sam and I arrived at Mom's apartment, I was told that my mom would never eat or drink again. She was semi-comatose.

I took Sam in to see his Grandma Jane. As he stood next to her bed, I sat down in a chair next to him. I held his hand. He got very quiet as he looked at her intently. Then he turned to me and said, "She is more there than here now, Mom."

"Yes, Sam, yes she is."

I was astounded by the clarity and wisdom of this seven-year-old.

On Friday, my sister-in-law Vicki brought over two pies. In her semi-comatose state Mom heard the word "pie" and perked right up. "Pie?!" and gave an enthusiastic "Yes!" when we asked if she would like some.

My sister Nancie exclaimed, "You better hurry up, Mom. I've already finished my first piece of pie!" My mom, who had only been speaking in one- and two-word sentences for the last two days called out to Nancie, "Nancie! You get in here. I want you to be where I can see you. I don't want you eating all my pie." When my brother Joel arrived with fried chicken, she asked for a chicken leg! Now, she only nibbled on the pie and chicken, but she was eating, teasing us and talking with us. She looked radiant. We drank it all in, honoring this special time we had been given.

By Saturday evening, her surge was over and we thought for sure she would die before morning. By Monday, she was in a coma with a temperature of one hundred and four. On Tuesday, her kidneys stopped functioning, and on Wednesday afternoon she died.

From the beginning of this two-week journey to my mom's death, I had told my sisters and brothers that I wanted to bathe my mom's body and prepare her for burial after she died. They looked at me with confusion and responded, "Do whatever you need to do, Kimberly, just don't expect us to be in there."

After Mom died, I asked the hospice nurse to help me bathe her. We washed her from head to toe with soapy water and then again with warm water infused with the essential oils of frankincense and rose. As we bathed her, my sister Kari came in to join us. Moments later, Jill came in and helped us wash Mom's hair. Then Jill dried and curled it, as she had done so many times over the years. Kari applied Mom's favorite lipstick to her lips. We dressed her in a lovely pair of silk pajamas that she had been saving for a special occasion. She looked absolutely beautiful. For the first time in three weeks, she looked like Mom. The rest of the family came in to join us. As we all stood around her bed, we felt intense joy at seeing Mom again and having the painful images of her last days replaced by these fresh images.

Mom's mouth hung open. We had tried to close it to no avail. My brother Rick expressed concern that we should get her to the funeral home ASAP or it may set that way. I assured him that it was OK; we had time. And there she lay, beautiful and peaceful, for the next three and a half hours so that her friends, nurses, and other family members could come and say their goodbyes.

Finally, as we were all gathered in the dining room, my brother Joel announced, "If you want to spend any more time with Mom, you better go in there now. The hearse just arrived." When I walked into her room to sit with her one last time, I gasped. Her mouth was closed, and she had a gentle smile on her face. I ran out of the room and yelled to my siblings, "Her mouth is closed!" They all came into the room, and we circled her bed in awe. What a gift! What a gift! These words echoed in our hearts as we joined hands and sang "Amazing Grace."

What a gift!
We joined hands and sang
"Amazing Grace."

Vigeland Sculpture Park
Oslo, Norway, 2010

Intentions

I SERVED AS A DOULA AT over twenty births. I created a kit that I took with me to each birth so that I would have tools to assist the mother in her laboring and birthing. As I prepared to be with my mom as she prepared to cross over, I brought a toolkit with me as well, but this was filled with energetic tools that I had been collecting. It was overwhelming to say goodbye to this woman who had birthed me into this world and who had devoted her life to raising eight children. I wanted her to be surrounded by love and support and to be ushered out of this world feeling complete.

I was aware of the land mine that family gatherings could be. I had few memories of large family gatherings where there were no arguments or drama. My brothers and sisters and I would be spending the next couple of weeks together. We have very diverse personalities. How could we navigate this emotionally charged time without lashing out at each other? How could I release old patterns within me so that I would not shrink and fall into old roles that no longer fit me? How could I bring my most authentic and loving self to this time?

In the dark of night, as I sat at my mom's bedside, both in the hospital and in her last days at home, I used my journal to ground myself, to find the words I longed to say to my mom and to my siblings, and to create a manifestation wheel to set my intentions for this potent time. The concept of a manifestation wheel had been described to me by Yvonne Kilcup, the co-founder of Intuitive Mind. This process helped to focus my attention, not on my fears, but on my hope. It grounded me in what was essential in this holy journey with my mom and siblings, and it provided internal focus, clarity, and strength.

I read my manifestation wheel every day as we journeyed with mom to her passing. It allowed me to stay focused and not get distracted by petty annoyances. It gave me the courage to ask for forgiveness when I was insensitive. It created a road map that helped me navigate my family landscape, and it guided me to live with authenticity amongst my family.

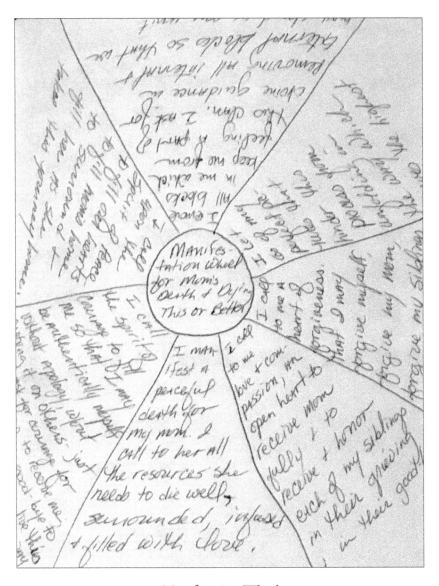

Manifestation Wheel
For My Mom's Dying, 2005

Exercise: Create a Manifestation Wheel

What is it you want to manifest in your life right now? A manifestation wheel can be helpful in focusing your energies for the big moments, for assisting you in big changes in your life and for magnetizing the deep desires of your heart.

Here are things to keep in mind:

- Use words that are positive and active.

  I manifest…
  I call to myself…
  I surround myself with…
  I invite…
  I let go of…
  I forgive…
  I remove…
  I release…
  I call upon…
  I create…

- Focus on qualities rather than specifics. This expands the possibilities. If we are too specific, we limit the possibilities. Focusing on the qualities allows for possibilities that may be beyond our imaginings.

Keep your manifestation wheel where you can see it and read it often.

- Gather a piece of paper and a pencil. Use colored pencils if you like.

- Make a circle in the center of the page. In this circle write your title: "A Manifestation Wheel For _____."

- Fill the blank with what it is you wish to manifest. In my case I filled the blank with, "Mom's Death and Dying."

- Under your title write "This or Better."

- Now draw lines from the outside of the circle to the edge of the page. This part of the process is intuitive for me. I create as many lines as feels right. Often there are five to nine lines creating spokes coming out from the circle. These spokes create triangular wedges.

- In each of the wedges write your intentions. Make sure to use action statements that are positive. I had seven spokes in my manifestation wheel for my mom's death. I wrote the following intentions in the triangles:

  - I manifest a peaceful death for Mom. I call to her all the resources she needs to die well, surrounded, infused, and filled with love.

  - I call to myself love and compassion, an open heart to receive Mom fully and to receive and honor each of my siblings in their grieving and in their goodbyes.

  - I call to myself a heart of forgiveness that I may forgive myself, forgive my mom, and forgive my siblings for any hurt, any harm we have done to each other.

  - I let go of my perfect pictures that hinder this process from unfolding in the way which serves the highest good.

  - I remove all blocks in me which keep me from being a part of this clan. I ask for Divine guidance in removing all internal and external blocks so that we may stand as one unit saying goodbye to Mom.

○ I call upon the Spirit of Peace to fill our hearts and to fill
Mom's home, to surround her as she takes this journey
home.

○ I call on the Spirit of Courage to fill me, so that I may be
authentically myself without apology, without pushing
it on others, just to be. I ask for courage for my siblings
to receive me, to say goodbye to Mom, and to live
this time in the way which serves them best. I ask for
courage for Mom as she steps over to the other side.

Use your manifestation wheel to help you focus your attention on your
dream and to create a road map that will help you navigate any doubt or
fear that may arise.

My Light Is Revealed

An endless source of Light, Love
Encouragement and Clarity
Is ready to support me
In each moment.

This light radiates
More fully into the world
As I inhabit my spirit.

As I move into my full potential.
Stagnant, protective,
Armored energy melts away.
I am grounded and infused.
I radiate loving kindness.

As I embody my whole and holy self,
A headdress of peace and clarity,
A cloak of love and healing
And a garment of fire and passion
Illuminate my spirit
And I am revealed.

♡ *Listen*

Breathe in your life.
Within you is the truth of who you are
and what you are called to do.
Make space in your life for silence
So that you can tune into the still, small voice within.
Follow that voice,
Rather than the clamoring voices that distract you
from your truth.
It will lead you to a life of passion, purpose and possibility and
To experiences beyond your imagining.

"Serve God's little ones with love.
You will know it is done with love if it is done with joy."
Mother Teresa

Statue of Mother Teresa at Marquette University, Wisconsin

Trust the Urgings of Spirit

THERE ARE PEOPLE IN THIS WORLD who become beacons of light for many. They stir something in us, and we find ourselves striving to take on a bit of the character they possess. For me, that person was Mother Teresa. She was the person I wanted to emulate. Throughout my young life, I imagined myself working next to her, filled with love and joy while caring for God's little ones. Something inside of me felt a deep kinship to those who were poor, those who were "untouchable," and those who were orphaned. Going to Calcutta to meet Mother Teresa and experience her work was my fantasy trip of a lifetime.

The year I turned thirty, this fantasy shifted to possibility when I learned that there was a L'Arche community in Calcutta, built on some of Mother Teresa's land. L'Arche is a community of persons with developmental disabilities (core members) and those who choose to live with them as family (assistants). I had become acquainted with L'Arche when I moved to Tacoma. Their Hilltop House, which was down the street from my church, soon became my second home. In L'Arche, I found the model of family that answered my childhood yearnings. Each member of the community is seen as valuable, lovable, and a vital contributor to the whole. Everyone is loved, respected and accepted with all their weaknesses and strengths, including me.

My long-held fantasy to travel to Calcutta to meet Mother Teresa and experience her work began to feel like more than a dream; it began to feel like a calling. For me, a calling is an urging of the spirit that propels me towards experiences for my soul's growth and for the benefit of something larger than myself. Often these callings feel impractical or nearly impossible, but beneath my practical mind is a quiet and strong voice that says, "Do it." I have come to trust this voice and to trust that all I need will be provided if only I say "Yes."

So, I said "Yes" to the call to go to Calcutta and meet Mother Teresa, and I made a plan to leave eight months later in October of 1990. I decided to take three months away from my massage practice in order to have plenty of time for this adventure. In order to do this, I would need to eliminate all debt, pay all of my monthly bills in advance, and by the end of August, have $1,500 in the bank to buy my airline ticket. I opened my calendar to August 31 and with a red pen, I wrote "$1,500." I placed my hand over that number, whispered a prayer of blessing and asked for clarity. Then I gave it over to God, trusting that if I was meant to go, everything I needed would be provided.

Next, I met with David Rothrock. David is the founder of the Tacoma L'Arche community. He served as the spiritual director for L'Arche Tahoma Hope in Tacoma and also at Asha Niketan, the L'Arche community in Calcutta. I asked David if he could help me to connect with Asha Niketan. He agreed and wrote a letter of introduction asking the community director if I could volunteer in their workshop where they made candles, tie-dye cloth, and cards. We waited for a response. After six weeks, he wrote again and still we received no reply. In 1990 that community did not have a phone or email. (Heck, even I didn't have email yet!) Snail mail was our only option, and it was unreliable in Calcutta. We waited and waited but no reply came.

The still, quiet voice within me encouraged me to go anyway. I figured that if I showed up at the L'Arche community in Calcutta and they did not need me, that there would be an organization in this, one of the poorest cities in the world, that could use a volunteer. I continued with my plans and focused on paying off my bills and getting money in the bank.

By August 30, I had paid all my bills and erased all debt, but I had only $200 in the bank. Although I had massage clients the next day, they were either on insurance, which meant I would not get paid for many weeks, or they were on account, which meant they had already paid for their session. I drove home from work that night feeling disappointed and questioning whether I was meant to go. The quiet voice within calmly and firmly whispered, "Just wait."

The next day, it rained money. I went to my P.O. Box and there was a check for me from an insurance company. My business associate, Katy, went to her P.O. Box and found another insurance check for me. Towards the end of the day, a man walked in and asked to buy ten gift certificates for his employees! At the end of the day, I was eighty-two cents short of my $1,500 goal. I found a dollar in my pocket; I slapped it on the desk and yelled, "I AM GOING!"

"Going where?" Katy asked.

"I am going to Calcutta to meet Mother Teresa!"

The validation I had asked for had been fulfilled. I was going to Calcutta.

Author's Note: In 2001, the government of West Bengal changed the English name of Calcutta to Kolkata to reflect its original Bengali pronunciation. When I was there in 1990, its common English name was Calcutta. For authenticity to the time and my experience, I refer to the city as Calcutta throughout *Spirit Embraced*.

Remove yourself from all distractions, breathe, and listen.
It is in stillness that we can best hear the voice of Spirit.

A Quiet Moment, Nepal, 1990

Follow the Quiet Voice Within

LISTENING TO THE VOICE OF MY spirit takes courage. It feels so much safer to allow my mind to dictate my life. But I don't want to play it safe; I am committed to following the voice of my spirit and to honor its nudging, no matter how frightening it feels. It is this commitment that has allowed me to change the paradigm of my life. It has demanded that I stay open to possibilities and required that I refuse to allow the inner critic or cerebral skeptic to manipulate my attention. These noisy voices can be like small children clamoring for attention. With clarity and strength, I tell them to stop and to go play elsewhere. I am busy and unavailable.

Thirty years ago, when I was a youth minister for a Catholic church, I read about the exercise in a youth ministry resource book. I lead the students through this exercise to help them tune into the voice of Spirit in their lives.

I asked for two volunteers. Volunteer A was the listener, and Volunteer B was the voice of Spirit. Volunteer A was blindfolded and twirled around to confuse their sense of direction. At the same time, Volunteer B chose a place across the room to stand while the other students moved the items in the room and even themselves to become obstacles between A and B. Once we were set, A was instructed to listen to and follow the voice of B and to safely get to B without running into or tripping over any of the people or objects that had been placed in their way. B was instructed to coach A forward, using a calm and steady voice. Slowly the two worked together…"Come forward two steps…Stop…Now turn to the right…Stop… Take three steps forward. Stop…" On and on the instructions went until A was standing directly in front of B. We all cheered and then took time to debrief this exercise. What was it like to follow the voice? What kind of focus did it require? Were you frightened or confident in its direction?

Next, I announced that there was another step to the exercise. Again, I blindfolded and twirled the same Volunteer A while Volunteer B found a new spot in the room and the other students created a new configuration of obstacles. Again, B was directed to guide A in a calm and steady voice that was no louder than the previous time. However, this time everyone in the room would also be giving directions. Every student could tell A what to do. They could use as loud or as quiet a voice as they wanted. They could give accurate or wrong directions.

Each time I did this exercise with groups of students, no matter how loud and outrageous the directions got, Volunteer A eventually became very still and would tune into that one quiet voice that had guided them before and followed it slowly and steadily to the goal. In the second debriefing, we explored the idea that there are many voices within and around us trying to get our attention and direct our path.

Our holy work is to take time in quiet to practice listening to our spirit and to tune into that still quiet voice within. The more we practice this, the more familiar we become with its voice and the easier it is to follow its direction even when the voices of our fear, anxiety, anger, skepticism, culture, family and friends try to drown it out.

Exercise: Listen

- Take a moment to recognize all the various voices within and around you that clamor for your attention.

- Now take many minutes to breathe deeply into your belly.

- As you breathe, allow your attention to go deeper than these surface voices.

- Allow the surface noise to fade away.

- Rest here in the quiet for a while and notice what arises.

Take time each day to stop, remove yourself from all distractions, breathe, and listen. It is in stillness that we can best hear the voice of Spirit.

Sweet Silence

Breathe deeply.

Deeper Still.

Breathe into the silence of your soul.

Breathe into this space for a moment

And feel it stretch into eternity.

Sweet silence,

Sweet solitude

Awaits you.

Breathe into the silence of your soul.
Breathe into this space for a moment
And feel it stretch into eternity.

Prayer Flags, Nepal, 1990

Negotiations

SOMETIMES I NEGOTIATE WITH SPIRIT. OFTEN, it feels like I'm being invited right up to the edge of all I know and am being asked to step into the unknown, and I am terrified. At times its whisperings seem so preposterous that I need confirmation that I heard correctly, so I tiptoe towards its invitation, rather than diving in. Other times, I dive right in, and it is only after I am fully immersed that I ask myself, "What was I thinking?"

Once my bills were paid and I had the money in the bank for my ticket to Calcutta, the enormity of the journey set in and shook me to my core. Here I was, a single, thirty-year-old woman traveling to a new continent by myself with no clear plans or contacts. What was I thinking? I was all in for going to Calcutta, yet I was also aware that I would feel more comfortable if there was someone on that continent expecting me.

To soothe my fear and create a safety net for myself, I enrolled in a yoga teacher training in Kathmandu, Nepal. Two months earlier, I had attended a Sacred Dance Institute in Portland, Oregon, where I participated in three one-hour yoga sessions. This was my first experience with yoga. The classes were led by Sushil, a yogi from Nepal. He invited the participants to enroll in his month-long yoga teacher training at his yoga center in Kathmandu in October. As my journey to Calcutta approached,

I convinced myself that after only three hours of accumulated yoga experience, I was ready for this yoga teacher training. I called the Yoga Center and left a message that I was registering for the training. Knowing that Sushil would be expecting me gave me the security I needed. I decided to stop in Bangkok for three days on my way to Nepal and planned to spend a week on the beach in Thailand at the end of my trip in order to process my entire experience before heading home. This plan left me six weeks in the middle to volunteer in Calcutta.

On October 31, 1990, my plane landed in Kathmandu. We landed on a small dirt airfield, and I took a bus into the center of the city. I got off the bus and felt like I had been transported back five hundred years in time. I walked along the streets with my huge backpack, exhilarated by the sights, sounds and smells: women in brightly colored saris, prayer wheels spinning, cows moving about the streets, meat markets with legs of animals hanging from the doorway, spices, fruits, and vegetables. I had a map of Kathmandu, and I hoped that I would be able to find my way to the Yoga Center, but the map was not much help. All the street signs were in Nepali, and my map was in English. When it became clear that I was not going to be able to locate the Yoga Center on my own, I enlisted the help of a bicycle rickshaw driver. When I arrived at the Yoga Center, Sushil was surprised to see me. It seemed he had not received my message. In his graciousness, he allowed me to join the class. My safety net had been an illusion. Whether I had gone straight to Calcutta or stopped in Nepal, no one was ever expecting me.

For the next month, I did yoga for eight and a half hours a day. By the end of the first day, I had quadrupled my lifetime yoga experience. I had never been very flexible, yet by the end of the third week of our training, I could sit on the ground, cross my feet at the ankles and bring my legs up and over my head. After thirty days, my body was transformed and I was astounded by the strength and power of my body.

Every day we meditated for two and a half hours. One night, during our fourth week of meditation, I felt a presence and heard a voice of intense love, calling my name and asking me to rest in this love. I kept moving into my head, trying to capture the experience so that I could write about it later but whenever I tried to analyze the experience, I would lose my connection to it. Finally, I let go of trying and simply sank into the presence of love. As I floated in this space, the love flowed through and around me and the most beautiful images filled my mind.

Later that night, Rick, a classmate, came into the women's dorm to find me. He sat down next to my bed and told me that as he was meditating, the Great Mother came to him filled with gentle, nurturing love for me. He said that she held and caressed me. After he left, I fell asleep astounded and grateful. My experience had been confirmed.

———————————— ◆ ————————————

As December approached, I prepared to leave Kathmandu for Calcutta. One of my classmates, Frieder, suggested we travel together. He was going to Puri, south of Calcutta. Frieder was a gentle, quiet-spirited man from Germany. Even though I respected and trusted him, I was so hungry for time alone that I declined and insisted that I would be fine. I wanted that time travelling between Kathmandu and Calcutta to myself. Over the next week, he continued to politely but pointedly ask me to travel together, and I continued to graciously decline. Having time alone was very important to me.

After our yoga training was completed, I took myself to a quiet mountain village for three days of solitude. Renewed and refreshed, on the bus ride back to Kathmandu, I was able to sink deeper than my hunger to be alone and heard with clarity that I needed to travel with Frieder to Calcutta.

For over forty-eight hours Frieder and I travelled, taking two buses and a train from Kathmandu to Calcutta. The first bus took us from Kathmandu to the border of Nepal. Arriving at 3:00 a.m., we paid a driver seventy-five cents to take us to the Immigration Office in his mule-drawn cart. At the Nepalese Immigration Office, we woke up the immigration officers who were sleeping together on two desks with a mosquito net hanging over them. One of the officers sat up, looked at our passports, stamped them and went back to sleep.

Carrying a backpack that felt like it weighed a hundred pounds, and with a full moon as our guide, we walked the mile across the border into India.

As we entered India, I felt like we had landed in Oz. We were greeted by the "Wizard," with a turban on his head and a twinkle in his eyes. Our Wizard sent us to a building across the way where our papers would be processed. We entered the empty office and waited. Moments later, to our surprise, the Wizard arrived. He asked us a series of questions regarding where we had been and what we had to declare. Satisfied with our answers, he sent us to another building where we were left to wait in the moonlight until the immigration officer got out of bed and arrived an hour later. He filled out a myriad of forms, made notations in many large books, and welcomed us to India.

As the sun, a magnificent ball of red and pink, greeted us, we boarded our second bus at 7:00 a.m. to Mustaphor where we would catch our train to Calcutta. As most of the windows in the bus were broken, I sat next to a glassless window as we travelled roads at ninety-seven kilometers per hour (equivalent to sixty miles an hour). With the wind streaming down my back, I wrapped myself as best I could in my shawl and used my backpack to shield me as I drank in the sights of India: rice, mustard, and sugar cane fields, banana trees, oxen and black boars running down the road, grass huts, and layers of smoke covering the landscape like fog. I was in India!

Six hours later, we boarded an all-night train to Calcutta. Our coach had a set of bunk beds and a bench. I slept on the top bunk, and Frieder slept on the bottom bunk. The bench was occupied by five men. Their big, dark eyes watched my every move. Throughout the night, when I would awaken, I would look down to find all ten eyes staring at me. Since leaving Kathmandu, I had not seen another Westerner. Our buses and trains had been filled with men. Very few women or children travelled with us and certainly, no women were traveling without a male escort. I now realized how important it was that I travelled with Freider and how vulnerable I would have been traveling alone. I was grateful for Freider's wisdom and insistence that we travel together and for the clarity of my quiet voice within that affirmed it.

After our long trip, Freider decided to stay in Calcutta to rest for a day before he continued on to Puri. When we arrived at Howrah Station, we found our way through the throng of people and took a *tuk tuk* into the city. A tuk tuk is a three-wheeled auto rickshaw meant to transport four people, including the driver, but often carries many more. It was not uncommon to see one or two people with just their feet inside the entrance to the tuk tuk and the rest of their bodies outside, hands holding on to the outside hood. The average vehicle goes six mph, so even a short trip of eight miles can take forty-five minutes or more. The tuk tuk dropped us off at the YMCA where we each got a room. I had a delicious hot shower and a nap. Refreshed and excited to be in Calcutta, I went in search of L'Arche.

As I was leaving the YMCA, the man behind the desk asked, "Where are you going?"

"I am going to find a community called "Asha Niketan" (Home of Hope).

"Oh, I know Asha Niketan!"

I was flabbergasted. Calcutta is a city of thirteen million people. At that time, the L'Arche community comprised only about twenty people. What were the chances of me meeting one of the few people who knew of this community? He carefully wrote out instructions on how to get to Asha Niketan. For three hours, I took two different tuk tuks through some of the poorest areas of Calcutta. I saw whole neighborhoods of homes made out of cardboard and plastic bags. Many families were living on the street meridians: cooking their food, relieving themselves, and sleeping right there on the side of the road. Everywhere I looked, there was someone begging for coins or food.

Finally, I arrived at the large, blue gate of Asha Niketan. As I stepped through the gate, I discovered four men standing right inside the gate.

Timidly I said, "I am looking for a man named Marc Laroche." Marc was serving as the director of the Calcutta L'Arche community and living at Asha Niketan with his wife and five children.

A tall Frenchman stepped forward saying, "I am Marc."

"Hi, Marc, my name is Kim Ebert. Have you ever heard of me?"

"No." He replied as he looked at me with confusion.

I clarified that David Rothrock had sent two letters of introduction to explain my deep connection to the Tacoma L'Arche community, and my desire to volunteer at the Asha Niketan workshop while I was in Calcutta.

Marc informed me that my letters had never arrived and invited me into his office where we could talk.

We had been talking for over an hour, when Marc turned to me and said, "Kim, we generally do not allow anyone from the West into our community for less than three months because it takes that long for them to acclimate."

My heart sank. Because of my time in Nepal, I only had six weeks left to offer him.

Then Marc looked at me and said, "We have been praying for over two weeks for God to send us someone. We are very short-staffed. I guess you are that someone. Would you be willing to come and live with us as well as volunteer in the workshop?"

I was delighted and humbled. I knew without a doubt that this trip had been designed and directed by the Divine. The next day, I moved in.

Feel the wonder of being on this earth
At this time
In a human body.
Let the wonder of your incarnation fill you.

Sunrise over the Himalayas

Beyond the Familiar

I WAS SCHEDULED TO ARRIVE AT Asha Niketan in the early afternoon. I spent the morning walking around Calcutta excited to explore this place I had dreamt of visiting since I was a young girl. I soon noticed however, that I had cut off my peripheral vision. The poverty was so intense that I could only take in that which was right in front of me: the young boy lying next to a building with no arms, the five-year-old boy sleeping on the sidewalk with an aluminum pot in front of him for people's spare change, the man whose legs were half the width of my arms, the man with his legs blown up with elephantiasis dragging himself across the street, the old woman whose sari was so tattered that her breasts were exposed, and the emaciated mother with a baby suckling on her bare breast, begging me to give her some coins. Years before, I had taken two groups of students down to the barrios of Tijuana on service trips. We worked in an orphanage, did repairs and clean up at a local school, worked in a feeding program for children, and even delivered meals to those who lived and worked in the garbage dumps. Yet even those experiences had not prepared me for the poverty before me in Calcutta.

When I arrived at Asha Niketan and got settled into my room on the second floor, I looked out the window and saw a palm tree blowing in the breeze and a beautiful red flower in the garden. I rested in the simplicity of

my room and enjoyed the gentle breeze. In time, I felt my spirit tug at me
to look beyond the safety of this home. Slowly, I looked past my comfort
zone and saw barbed wire above the wall that surrounded Asha Niketan
and ragged buildings, tattered rooftops, bicycle rickshaws, roaming pigs
and hordes of dogs just beyond its walls.

Throughout my time in Calcutta, that quiet voice within encouraged
me to stay present, to stay in my body, to feel the emotions that came up.
The temptation was to stay in my head and to try to shut down anything
uncomfortable that was arising. The challenge was to breathe into the
edges, beyond my familiar.

Exercise: Grounding

It is easy to shut down our body wisdom and to give our mind the currency of our attention, as if all we are is encased in our brain. As we center our consciousness in our minds, and exclude the wisdom of our gut, heart, and core, there is too much energy in our heads and much of our energy floats above us. This causes us to feel scattered, overwhelmed, and/or highly analytical.

We are our most powerful when our spirit is embodied and our energy is flowing throughout our body. This gives us stability and fosters clarity, and feelings of peace, even in the midst of challenges.

In 2004, I had a profound session with a gifted healer, Nancy Rebecca. Nancy and her partner Yvonne Kilcup are the founders of the Intuitive Mind Center in Tacoma, Washington. I immersed myself in the courses they offered to expand my ability to trust my deep intuition. The following exercise comes from my studies with Nancy and Yvonne. This grounding process provides support as we move beyond the edges of our familiar. It brings our energy down into our body, helps us to break through the static of our mind chatter, and powerfully connects us to the energy of the earth.

- Sit with your feet firmly planted on the floor.

- Close your eyes and take a few deep breaths.

- As you feel yourself settle into this time, imagine an energetic cord that starts just below your ovaries if you are a woman, and beginning just below your testes if you are a man.

- Imagine this cord growing and moving down through the floor, down into the earth, and then imagine it going, down into the center of the earth.

Many people imagine this cord as roots that they tie to the center of the earth. I imagine mine as the pneumatic tube I use at the drive-through at my bank. I send this tube to the center of the earth and secure it there with two huge bolts. Allow your imagination to create an image of the grounding cord that works for you.

- As your grounding cord goes deeper into the earth, feel your spirit move into your body.

- Now secure the cord to the center of the earth.

- As you secure your grounding cord into the center of the earth, feel your spirit fully lock into your earth suit.

- Now feel green earth energy come up from the earth and flow through your feet, up your legs, and into your pelvis.

- Any excess earth energy that your body does not need will be returned down your grounding cord.

- As you allow earth energy to run through your body, feel the support of the earth. It is a gift to walk this earth. Feel the wonder of being on this earth at this time in a human body. Let the wonder of your incarnation fill you.

As you move towards the unknown and unfamiliar and fear or anxiety threaten to overtake you, simply imagine yourself releasing these feelings down your grounding cord. Give them over to the earth and allow the earth to transmute these powerful feelings into something useful for the planet.

Once you have developed this process and have an image of your grounding cord, this process can be a fifteen-minute meditation or it can be a twenty-second exercise you do as you move through your day.

- Grounding cord secured to the center of the earth…Check

- Spirit fully locked into my body…Check

- Earth energy coming up through the center of my feet and flowing up through my legs filling my pelvis…Check

- Excess energy going down through my grounding cord…Check

- Feeling supported and grounded…Check

The Great Amen

The Great Amen
Takes root in me.
Growing deep.
Shifting, changing
The landscape of my life.
As I let go of safe ground,
My insides quake.
The land beneath my feet
Rearranges itself,
Leaving me standing in
Uncharted territory.
Gingerly, I walk this new landscape,
Uncertain, uncomfortable with
the unfamiliar path ahead.
Deep and dark rumblings within me
Echo the Great Amen.

*Bapi was a beautiful soul
who curled into my heart and
took up residence there.*

Bapi, 1990

Edges and Boundaries

DESPITE MY ENTHUSIASM, IT TURNED OUT Marc Laroche was right: It took me a while to settle in. Everything felt foreign to me. I slept on a bed that was a piece of plywood with a thin futon mattress on top and a mosquito net overhead. We sat on the floor in the dining room to eat our meals; there were no chairs. We ate our food with our fingers; there were no utensils. We touched people and food with our right hand only; our left hand was reserved for cleaning ourselves. We used a small bucket of water and our left hand to attend to all bodily functions and hygiene; there was no toilet paper. The food was so spicy hot that I could barely eat it and my body revolted every time I tried.

I lived with seven developmentally disabled men (core members) and two male assistants. The men all lived in the dorm on the first floor. Because I was the only female assistant, I had the women's dorm, on the second floor, all to myself.

As a massage therapist, I touch people for a living, and touch is an important form of communication for me. Culturally, it was inappropriate for me to touch these men in any way. Even a touch on an arm as we spoke or sitting next to each other close enough for our knees to touch was unacceptable.

Most of the men I lived with spoke Bengali. As the weeks progressed, I became frustrated because I was not learning enough Bengali to understand or to communicate with these precious men. Worse yet, one of the core members spoke English as his primary language, and I found myself avoiding him because I was even more frustrated that I had a hard time understanding him!

Bapi was a beautiful soul who curled into my heart and took up residence there. He was one of the core members. Bapi broke through my ego because he spoke his own language—gibberish. Because there was no way I could understand his words, I didn't try. Instead, Bapi taught me how to listen beyond the words. Each night, after dinner, he and I would sit on the veranda. Bapi would tell me story after story. I learned to listen to his tone, watch his expressions, read his body language, and to respond to what I heard. If his eyes were twinkling and a giggle broke through, I laughed with him. If he was sad, my tears flowed with his. When he was angry, I listened with compassion.

Georgie taught me how to express myself without words or touch. After I had been living in Asha Niketan for about a month, Georgie, a core member who spoke Bengali, received a message that his brother Lenny was very ill and was dying. Naturally, Georgie was very upset and throughout our evening prayer he cried. I did not know what to do. I could not go and hug him or put my arms around him because that would be culturally inappropriate. I had no words to soothe his pain. After our chapel time, I went and sat in the dining room with my back against the wall near the doorway. I closed my eyes and opened my hands on my lap. In my heart I said, "Georgie, if you need me, I am here." Georgie came into the dining room and sat down in front of me. We were both sitting "crisscross applesauce," and he sat as close to me as possible without touching. I opened my eyes and looked into Georgie's and sent all the love and compassion I could into his eyes. Together we cried. Without touching or words, my tears of compassion met his deep grief.

On my last day in Calcutta, I took my backpack to the gate. All these precious men that I lived with for six weeks gathered at the gate to say their goodbyes. As I looked around, I discovered that Bapi was not there. While my taxi waited, I went back inside to look for him. I found him sitting on the veranda. I asked him to please come out with the rest of us to say our goodbyes. After much coaxing, he slowly walked towards the gate with me. His shoulders were sagging and a deep frown creased his face. When we stepped through the gate, Bapi stopped, pointed at the house and let me have it. Even though I had taken a day or two each week away from Asha Niketan to stay in the city and work in Mother Teresa's facilities, Bapi knew this leaving was different and he was angry. He knew I was leaving Asha Niketan for good. I looked deeply into his eyes. As our tears flowed, I told him that I loved him, that I was grateful for all he had taught me, and that I would always carry him in my heart.

Over the years, there have been a handful of times when I have awakened from a dream in which I was visiting with Bapi. The dreams feel so real; I wake up filled with love and joy. Bapi taught me how to listen, even as I dream.

————————◆◆————————

Life inside the gates of Asha Niketan felt quite foreign to me, and life outside those gates took me to my very edges where I felt foreign even to myself. I had assumed myself a compassionate and loving person, one who strives to be of service whenever possible. Calcutta challenged these assumptions about myself.

The afternoon I moved into Asha Niketan, one of the assistants offered me a glass of water. I politely declined. He assured me that it had been filtered and took me into the kitchen to see the filtration system. It was a two-tiered metal container. I smiled as he drank a glass of water to show me how it was safe to drink. I ignored the quiet voice within that cautioned me not to drink this water. Instead, I listened to and followed the loud, shaming voice that told me not to be rude, and timidly said, "Thank you. I would love a glass of water." Late that evening, I woke up with a fever of one hundred and two and extreme digestive distress. I had a parasite.

After I contracted the parasite, eating meals at Asha Niketan became unbearable. The food was so spicy hot that after every meal, I had to run straight to the bathroom. Marc asked our dear cook, Mashima, to make me a special meal that had no spices added. Mashima was generous of heart and agreed to add this extra task to her day. I am certain that she could not imagine eating something without the delicious Indian spices, so she added extra salt instead. This made my food so salty that it tasted like it had been cooked in sea water. Within a day or two, I asked Mashima to just feed me what she fed the others. The spicy, hot food was much more palatable than the salty food, even if it continued to leave me in digestive distress.

Every time Marc needed someone to run into the city for an errand, I would quickly volunteer. The drive into the city involved auto taxis and buses filled to overflowing and each trip required at least three hours of round trip transportation time, but I had found a Chinese restaurant that served a chicken and rice dish that did not make me sick. Any chance that was presented to go into the city and fill up on chicken and rice, I took gratefully.

On one such errand, I walked into my favorite Chinese restaurant, sat down, and opened the menu. As I browsed the menu, an image slapped me in the face. In that moment I realized that as I walked into the restaurant, there was an old woman, a beggar, sitting on the steps of the restaurant. I stepped right over her and through the doorway of the restaurant and did not acknowledge her in any way, not to myself, nor to her. I simply stepped over her and went to have my meal.

This realization shook me to my core. My spirit urged me to recognize my limitations. I was a kind and compassionate woman and yet there were limits to my compassion. When walking or driving through the streets of Calcutta, I felt assaulted by the needs of others—needs I could not possibly meet. I was frustrated that I was not a miracle worker who could magically make it all go away and it was painful for me to recognize how many times I had failed to offer even the most basic of human dignities.

This encounter with the old woman on the steps of the restaurant revealed to me my growth edge. It challenged me to open myself and dare to look at the people who crossed my path. Even if I could not meet their needs, I could acknowledge our shared humanity. I began to understand more fully that it was possible and important to honor both my boundary and their humanity. Neither of us needed to be invisible.

This encounter also invited me to recognize the parts of myself that were begging for my crumbs of acceptance. I was challenged to offer them my presence and compassion, rather than walking over them and ignoring their cries as I moved toward the more comfortable places within myself.

I imagine myself as the Great Mother
holding them in my arms and tenderly whispering,
"I love you and I am so sorry."

Nepalese Grandmother, 1990

Connect Spirit to Spirit

Bapi and Georgie taught me how to communicate in new and unexpected ways. And the old woman at the steps to the restaurant cultivated within me an understanding that it is imperative for my spiritual well-being that I honor both my boundaries and the shared humanity of those on my path. These lessons have been invaluable as I navigate life's challenges.

There have been times when I have chosen to limit contact with a family member or friend for my emotional and spiritual well-being. This decision is always difficult for me because I value loyalty and faithfulness in my relationships. I have discovered, however, that I do not need to disconnect spiritually just because I am creating a physical and emotional boundary. I can connect spirit to spirit. This allows me to honor my Self and to actively stay connected to others on a soul level.

Sometimes distance has made it impossible to be with a loved one who is suffering. Connecting spirit to spirit allows me to move beyond the limits of time and space to actively offer comfort and healing.

At times, I am overwhelmed by the suffering in the world and feel inadequate to make an impact. Each natural disaster, each new species threatened with extinction or the endless sufferings of war leave me feeling helpless. I release my feelings of inadequacy and move into my connection to all of life and offer my support and love.

Of course, I still discover long forgotten parts of myself waiting to be acknowledged and loved. However, I can stay connected to myself as an adult, in this time and space, and meet the hurting one within with love and compassion.

To accomplish this, I use the following exercise:

Exercise: I Love You and I Am Sorry

- Sit with your feet on the floor and your eyes closed.

- Take a few deep breaths.

- Now imagine your loved one in front of you.

- Look deeply into their eyes.

- If it feels right, tenderly cup their face in your hands.

- Feel your heart expand and fill with love, acceptance, and compassion for this person.

- When you are ready, say to them, "I love you and I am so sorry."

- Surround them in light.

- Continue to breathe deeply.

- When it feels complete, open your eyes and take a long cleansing breath.

It is important to note that the expression of "I am so sorry" is an expression of deep compassion for what they are experiencing, rather than an admission of guilt.

I do this practice anytime a loved one from whom I am separated comes into my consciousness. Not only does this practice feed our connection, but it also stops the whirling in my brain. It gives me something active to do, rather than hyper focusing on any concerns I may have.

I also do this exercise when I am overwhelmed by the suffering in the world and feel inadequate to make an impact. I imagine the people suffering from the latest hurricane, or the Orca mother who carried her dead calf on her back for seventeen straight days, or the people affected by the war in Syria, and I imagine myself as the Great Mother holding them all in my arms and I tenderly whisper, "I love you and I am so sorry." Then I imagine golden light showering them, healing them, strengthening them and bringing them peace.

Furthermore, I use this exercise when I recognize a part of my own Self yearning to be acknowledged.

- I imagine her standing in front of me.

- I look deeply into her eyes.

- I tenderly cup her face in my hands.

- I feel my love, acceptance, and compassion for her.

- I breathe into the opening in my heart and I say, "I love you and I am so sorry."

- And I surround her in golden light until every cell of her being sparkles.

Are there people who are unhealthy for you to be around, but that you want to stay connected to on a soul level? Are there people in your life that you cannot be with because of the limits of space and time? Does the world's pain overwhelm you? Are there parts of yourself that you ignore and pretend are not there? Take some time now to consider these questions. Explore this process of connecting spirit to spirit with those to whom you cannot be physically present but with whom you long to offer your love and compassion.

Temple of Protection

Staggering abundance.

Too much stuff

in the way

of feeling.

Hands reach out

Wanting, wanting,

too much from me.

I crawl inside my temple of protection.

Deep inside,

Where your wanting cannot touch me

And where for a moment—

if I do not breathe—

I can block out the cries for freedom.

"Love others as
God loves you.
God bless you,

Mother Teresa, MC
23/12/90"

Mother Teresa and Me
Calcutta, 1990

A Gentle Guide and an Undeniable Force

OFTEN TIMES THE VOICE OF OUR spirit is a gentle whisper guiding our way. Other times, it is insistent and clear and so powerful that there is no doubt what we are to do. One morning in Calcutta, I experienced Spirit coaxing me along, gently offering me directions. Later that evening, I experienced the undeniable force of its clarity.

Each week, I spent at least twenty-four hours away from Asha Niketan. On my first day away, I went to one of the oldest neighborhoods in South Calcutta and volunteered at Kalighat, Mother Teresa's Home for the Dying and Destitute. Kalighat is a free hospice for the poor that is housed in an old abandoned Hindu temple to the goddess Kali. It is a large building with cement walls and floors. There are two main sections: The men's ward and the women's ward. Each side holds fifty beds. I was assigned to the women's ward. There was bed after bed of women suffering, lying on their single cot with a thin plastic mattress. The Sisters and volunteers fed, washed, and cared for each of them. The needs seemed so huge and my capabilities felt so small. I felt helpless and believed that unless I could be there for many days or many weeks, I had little to offer.

As I sat at the edge of one cot and visited with the woman lying there, one of the Sisters came up to me. She had learned that I was a massage therapist, and she wondered if I could come and massage the woman in bed forty-eight. I was grateful to have a job I could fulfill. I enthusiastically said "Yes!" Bed forty-eight was set against the far wall. Together we gently turned the woman's frail body so that her back was available to me. As we moved her, tears of agony slid down her cheeks. I saw that her back was covered in bed sores and there was very little skin between the open sores. Nothing in my training had prepared me for this. Once again, I felt completely unprepared for what it was I was being asked to do. I closed my eyes and said a prayer. I asked Jesus to work through my hands and to show me what to do. Slowly, I began to stroke her energy field, about a foot above her body, whispering the prayer of my heart, "Use me, Lord. Use these hands to give her some relief." I listened and followed, massaging her field, stroking her hair, gently touching any skin that was not covered in sores. Her breath deepened, her eyes closed, and she fell asleep. With Spirit's gentle guidance, I had accomplished what I thought I could not do.

That evening, I went to Mother Teresa's Mother House for prayer. The chapel is a large room on the second floor. One side of the room is reserved for the nuns. The other side is for visitors. We were encouraged to take a plastic rosary from the box and to find a place to sit. I sat on the floor next to the aisle in the hopes that I would be able to get a glimpse of Mother Teresa. One of the nuns rose to welcome us and told us that Mother Teresa had just returned the night before from a trip to Yugoslavia. It was in that moment that I realized that I could have travelled all this way and she might not have been here. She has communities all over the world, yet in my naiveté, I had assumed that if I came to see her, she, of course, would be here.

As the nuns began their procession into the chapel, I was filled with excitement and awe. Here I was in Calcutta in the chapel of Mother Teresa's Mother House.

Then I saw her and my eyes filled with tears. She came down the aisle and chose her seat right across the aisle from me! I didn't pray at all. I just watched this holy woman next to me. I expected to see lightning bolts coming from her head or a large halo around her. Instead, I witnessed a woman who seemed more like a grandmother than the Wonder Woman she was in my mind. Humbly, she sat praying her rosary. I was struck by how ordinary she was.

After prayer, Mother Teresa announced that Confession would be available here in the chapel. I stood, and with many of the guests, I filed out of the chapel. Instead of going down the stairs with those who were leaving, I went around the corner and down the hallway, where no one could see me. I stood with my back against the wall and debated over what I was going to do. There were so many good reasons to slip out. I had met two young women from Scotland that afternoon who had invited me to join them for tea. If I stayed for Confession, I would miss having tea with them. They spoke English and I could understand them! They were women and I was living in a house filled with men. And yet, I felt an urge to go to Confession. It was just a couple of weeks before Christmas, this day had been intense, and I had a lot to process. I did not like going to Confession to a priest I did not know and trust. And I really wanted to meet those women for tea!

As I stood in that hallway, arguing with myself, Mother Teresa came walking toward me. I have no idea how she knew I was there. She came right up to me, looked deeply into my eyes, and said, "So, you are going to Confession?"

"Yes, Mother!" I said shaking my head up-and-down emphatically.

How could I possibly say "No" to Mother Teresa?!!

She took my arm in hers and walked me back to the chapel. Once we entered the chapel, she pointed at the top of my head and said, "The line for Confessions will form here."

With amazement, I wondered what I had ever done to warrant being ushered to Confession by Mother Teresa! That day Spirit had made it very clear that it was important I go to Confession and skip the tea.

Mother Teresa invited us to end each day by looking at our hand and seeing written on our fingers the words, "You Did It Unto Me."

Calcutta, 1990

A Prayer for the End of the Day

O N NEW YEAR'S EVE, MOTHER TERESA invited thirty of us volunteers to join her at the Mother House. She sat on a simple chair and we sat around her on the floor. I sat at her left foot, so close that I was able to examine her bunions. I felt deep compassion for the pain I knew they must cause her. Like a grandmother with all her little ones at her feet, we listened to her stories, wisdom, and wit. I had no memories of having a grandmother, but as I sat at Mother Teresa's feet, I felt like a grandchild.

Mother Teresa invited us to end each day by looking at our hand and seeing written on our fingers the words, "You did it for me…You did it to me…You did it with me." And to ask ourselves, "What did I do for Jesus today…to Jesus…with Jesus?

Exercise: You Did It Unto Me

I use this process in the evening to examine my day and to focus my life. I believe that Jesus is every person and that the Divine is in all of creation. As I ask these questions, I am examining how I lived my life to, with, and for others. I am examining how I honored the Divine within myself. Because I believe that God lives in every cell of my being, I also use these questions to explore how I live in relation to my own body.

What did I do TO my body today?

Did I listen to its needs and respond compassionately?

Did I give it food and drink that was nourishing, or did I fill it with foods that have little nutritional value and make it difficult for each cell to do its job optimally?

Did I give it rest or push it beyond reason?

What did I do WITH my body today?

Did I use it to reach out to others or to push them away?

Did I allow myself to express myself with my body?

Did I sing out with joy, giggle with glee, dance with delight, moan into my sadness or run out my frustration?

Did I greet my beloveds with open arms?

Did I make eye contact with those who crossed my path this day?

What did I do FOR my body today?

Did I exercise?

Did I move and stretch or did I stagnate my energy by staring at a screen all day?

Did I participate in activities that promote its healing?

Jesus is not the image of the Holy that holds meaning for everyone. These questions can be asked and will hold the same power with any name you choose for the Divine.

What did I do for Love? What did I do to Love? What did I do with Love...for the Universe...for the Great Mother...for El Shaddai...for the Beloved...for the Goddess...for Mother Earth and Father Sky...?"

As I worked with the woman in bed forty-eight, I stayed, even in the midst of my fear and feelings of inadequacy, for Love. I approached her, recognizing in her the Beloved and I massaged her field, face, and head with deep love. I invited and allowed the power of Christ to infuse and direct me.

Take time now to look at your hand. See the words written on your fingers:

> You
>
> Did
>
> It
>
> To
>
> Me

Using your words for the Divine, ask yourself,

What did I do to ——————?

What did I do with ——————?

What did I do for ——————?

Record your answers in your journal.

Allow your discoveries to guide and inform your life.

Breathe in Deeply

Breathe in.
Breathe out.
Breathe in deeply.
Breathe out.
Imagine yourself whole,
Holy.
Breathe in.
Breathe out.
Be present
To your Self.
Take your breath more deeply
Into your core.
Feel it fill every nook and cranny
Of the inner cavern of yourself.
As you breathe,
Feel your breath activate your cells
With golden light.
Feel yourself supported,
Nourished,
Enlivened
By this community of cells activated
in this moment of Peace.
Breathe in.
Breathe out.
Breathe.

❧ Manifest

Manifestation is not about magically making your wishes come true.
It is about listening deeply to the voice of your spirit,
trusting the deep desire of your heart,
and faithfully moving towards the dream.
It is a process that requires your full, "Yes!"
and consistent movement towards the vision.

I choose to trust the voice of my spirit.
I breathe into this trust and step into the
unknown with a full-hearted "Yes!"

❖

My Yes Takes Flight
Moclips, Washington, 2010

My Manifestation Process

LISTENING TO THE URGINGS OF MY spirit takes courage, openness, and tenacity. I must refuse to allow my inner critic or skeptic to manipulate my focus. These voices can be like a gaggle of children, clamoring for my attention. With clarity and strength, I tell them to stop and go play elsewhere. I am busy and unavailable.

Say Yes

I choose to trust the voice of my spirit. I breathe into this trust and step into the unknown with a full-hearted "Yes!" As I work in harmony with my spirit, I discover that it guides me toward what is most essential and meaningful in my life. I trust that everything I need will be provided and that wherever my spirit is leading me is for my greatest good.

Make a plan

I identify core goals that are required in order for my dream to be fulfilled. When I said yes to Calcutta, I identified two core goals that I needed to focus on to bring my dream into reality: all of my debt needed to be paid off and I needed $1,500 in the bank by the end of August to buy my airline ticket. I was an active participant in achieving these goals. I worked towards them each day and changed my spending habits to support my mission.

Focus on the qualities, rather than the specifics

When I am trying to manifest my heart's deep desires, I focus on the qualities of the manifestation rather than the specifics. For example, if I were looking for a new job, I might create a list like this:

I call forth a career in a company or organization with a mission and practices that I deeply respect, which

Utilizes my talents and calls forth my gifts,

Provides a positive work environment,

Encourages space and free time to nurture family relationships,

Compensates me with all the resources I need to support my family, provide for my children's education, travel for leisure, and prepare for my retirement.

The specifics can get in the way. I can only imagine what I already know. Perhaps there is something beyond my imagining waiting to come through. When I focus on the qualities rather than the specifics, it leaves room for possibilities that I could not have imagined to come forth.

Give it over to the Divine

I ritualize giving my dream and goals over to the Divine. This helps me to release any fear, hesitation or anxiety, and to trust that something greater than my ego is at work. It is an act of letting go and surrendering to trust.

If it's a habit I want to break or something I need to release to live my life with more authenticity and freedom, I write it on a piece of paper, pray a blessing over it, and then burn it in a fire pit, fireplace, or sink as a concrete example of my release.

If it is something I wish to draw to me that is time sensitive, I write it on the due date in my calendar, circle it with a colored pen, and say a prayer over it.

When I said "Yes" to the dream of going to Calcutta, I wrote my goal of $1,500 on my calendar, circled it with a red pen, and prayed a blessing over it to ritualize the giving over of the dream to the Divine. From that moment on, I was not worried about whether I should or should not go; I was confident that it all would be made clear. My deep confirmation came on August 31, when the $1,500 for my ticket was provided.

Wait and watch with joyful anticipation

Once I say a complete and full "Yes!" to a deep desire of my heart, then I wait with playful anticipation. I keep my eyes and heart open for surprising ways the path to my dream is revealed. I enjoy this part of the process a lot. I leave all anxiety behind and I trust.

In 1993, I found a house I wanted to buy. I was a self-employed, single woman with little savings. The house I found needed cosmetic work, but it had good bones. I knew I could afford the payments, and most importantly, it was a house that would allow me to participate more fully in the community I loved. I said "Yes!", signed the sales contract, paid the earnest money and headed to my office. I would need $5,000 at closing which was only six weeks away.

At my office, I met with a potential new renter named Kay. Kay and I were acquaintances who met one day after Mass. I was wearing a lavender t-shirt designed with a mandala encircled by a woman. A quote about the Divine Feminine was woven into the mandala. Kay came right up to me and, with a twinkle in her eye, said, "Any woman who wears a t-shirt like that in a place like this is a woman I want to know." We giggled together and introduced ourselves. Now months later, Kay was meeting with me to see about renting space in my office for her massage therapy practice.

As we sat down, I was bubbling with excitement. I blurted out, "I just put down earnest money on a house!" I then told her all about the house and the neighborhood. With confidence and glee, I said, "Now I just need to find $5,000 in the next six weeks for my down payment. I have no idea where that money is going to come from, but I know that this is my house and somehow the money will come!"

Kay looked at me and said, "Kim, I have $5,000 that I can loan to you."

I was astonished. By the time she left my office, we had created and signed a contract and payment plan for my $5,000 loan for the house. We also signed a rental agreement for Kay to rent my office. Her rent would provide the added income I would need to paint and update my new home.

Be prepared to take unexpected turns

My dreams and goals do not always unfold in the way that I expect. Opportunities can come when and where I least expect them. My best-laid plans may not be the best plan. I must stay open and flexible. My mantra for my dreams is always, "This or better."

When I paid the earnest money on my house, I believed that I could and would come up with the $5,000 that I needed for the down payment. I did not know how I would get this money and yet I did not flinch. I knew I could do it. I allowed my imagination to present creative options: I could do a marketing campaign for my office and sell packages of multiple sessions; I could increase my work hours; I could take on a second job. When Kay said she had $5,000 she could loan me, it was the last thing I had expected, yet, I knew this was the perfect solution. The payment schedule we created suited both of our needs. This solution was beyond my imagining. When it presented itself, I trusted the clarity I felt within and jumped at the opportunity.

Say Yes again and again

One yes can lead to many opportunities. The invitation is to stay awake, stay open, say "Yes!" again and again, then watch the magic unfold.

In this section, I will share with you how my "Yes" to going beyond the edge of comfort in the midst of the deaths of three loved ones, led me to say "Yes" to committing to my spirit's need to reconnect with life. This, in turn, led to a "Yes" to fulfilling an item on my bucket list, which then led to so much more.

Hungry Heart

Opening the door,
My Hungry Heart
Cries out.
My Soul Responds,
"I am here."

My soul responds,
"I am here."

Maui, 2018

Lean In to the Adventures of Spirit

"WOULD YOU GO TO THE OPRAH Show with me? I need to do something fun for my spirit."

This is the question I posed to my dear friend, Cathy, in the spring of 2003. She responded with an enthusiastic, "Yes!" and the adventure began.

For six months, my family had been walking intimately and intensely with death. The deaths of my mother-in-law, Jerry, my beloved friend, Bob, and my dear friend's daughter, Etta, had rocked our world. My spirit was yearning to reconnect to life.

In early September, we learned that my mother-in-law's cancer had spread throughout her body. As we sat with her in the doctor's office, he told her that there was nothing they could do. They were shifting their focus to comfort care.

In October, our dear friend, Bob died. Bob had Down syndrome and lived in L'Arche. He spent holidays at our home, always called me Mary, and loved to sing, "Home on the Range." Like Bapi, he took up a permanent residence in my heart. As Bob aged and his physical and psychological needs increased, he was moved into a care facility.

One Sunday afternoon, Niko, Sam, and I went to visit Bob. As we stopped at the front desk to check in, the nurse looked at us with dismay and said, "He just died."

I looked at her with confusion and asked, "What do you mean 'He just died?'"

She said, "One minute" and returned to a phone call and said, "Yes doctor, I am calling to let you know that Bob Emmerson just died."

Niko took Sam and settled in across from the nurse's station in front of a public phone. He began the task of calling all who loved Bob. I walked down the long hallway to Bob's room to sit with his body, to whisper prayers of gratitude for his friendship, and to pray for his spirit's swift and easy crossing. After a while, Niko and I switched places and I made calls and he sat at Bob's side. As we switched places for the third time, I noticed Sam following me. I stopped in my tracks and asked, "Do you want to see Bob?" Sam responded with a firm and clear "Yes." I took his hand and together we walked into Bob's room.

At four years old, this was Sam's first experience of death. As we stood next to Bob's bed, I asked, "Are you scared?"

He replied, "No. Just sad. He's dead, Mom."

"We can see his body is still here, but can you feel that his spirit is gone?"

"Yes," he replied.

When the phone calls were completed, Niko and Sam left me alone with Bob and went to have hamburgers nearby. When they returned, Sam came to me and took my hand. He looked into my eyes and, with conviction and compassion, said, "He can't talk, Mom. He's dead. He can't talk." A few weeks later, Sam went to his first memorial service. As a parent, I wanted to shield Sam from this early initiation of death, but life had other plans. Sam was clear and curious. My job was to model a healthy relationship with death and dying and to answer his many questions as they came up.

———————◆◆———————

A few days before Thanksgiving, my dear friend Pennye's sixteen-year-old daughter, Etta, died in a bus crash while she was studying in Bolivia. I sat with Pennye as she planned Etta's funeral. When she asked me to preside at Etta's service, I could barely breathe. I could not imagine fulfilling this big task. I told her that we were leaving to see Niko's mom, Jerry, the next day and I did not know how close she was to her own passing. I did not want to commit to presiding at the funeral and then have to cancel. I promised to help her find someone.

Early the next morning, I called our friend, Susan, who is an ordained minister and works in the hospice field. She told me she could not do it. And then, without knowing that Pennye had asked me to preside, Susan asked, "Kim is there any reason you can't do it?" I explained that we were traveling over the mountains to visit Jerry in Eastern Washington, and I was not one hundred percent sure that I could come back for the funeral.

Shortly after my call with Susan, my friend Joanna called. She had just awakened and wanted to tell me about an incredibly vivid dream she had had about Etta's funeral. Joanna said, "The weird thing was, Kim, that in my dream, you were presiding at her funeral." Joanna had no idea that Pennye had asked me to preside.

The final push from Spirit came when we arrived at Niko's parents' home. Jerry was doing well and looked more vibrant than we had seen her in weeks. I called Pennye and told her I would preside. In three different ways, Spirit had nudged me and said, "Do this." Finally, I set my fear aside and said, "Yes."

———————◆●◼———————

In December, we got the call that Jerry would most likely die within two weeks. Niko and I agreed that he only had one chance to do this, to be with his mom as she journeyed to her death. He would not get a chance to go back and do it over. What could be more important than spending these last weeks with his mom? Niko managed to be released from work and went to be with her. Those two weeks turned into three months. He spent half of each week in Eastern Washington with his mom and then came home for the other half of the week to be with Sam and me. In early March, as Niko snuggled next to her, Jerry passed away.

Grief was ever-present to us. At times, the weight of it seemed overwhelming, and I knew I needed to do something to keep me connected to the joy of living. I thought about my bucket list and said "Yes!" to the Oprah show.

What is it that nourishes and energizes
your whole and holy Self?

My Circle of Joy, 2011

Discover What Brings the Spirit Joy

IN THE MIDST OF MY GRIEF, I knew I had to do something to reconnect with life and to feed my spirit. Gratefully, my relationship with my spirit was strong, and I could move towards the things that would help bring balance and renewed joy in the midst of this painful time.

To draw joy into our lives, we must be in touch with what brings us joy. What are the imaginings that lift our spirits, that fill us with life, and that come back to us again and again? One of the first steps in manifesting is having a clear picture of what it is that we want to draw into our lives.

Over forty percent of my clientele have been seeing me for over twenty-five years. As a result, I have journeyed with many of them through their parenting years, marriages, careers, and into the transition times of retirement and the empty nest. For many of them they entered this period with confusion over what was next for them. Who were they without that career? How did they want to spend their time now that their children had been launched? With one such client, I asked, "What is it that brings your spirit joy?" She shook her head and said, "I have no idea anymore. My life has been focused on my kids and my husband and their needs for so long, I don't know who I am. The things that brought me joy before motherhood do not interest me anymore."

I used the Spirit Board exercise to guide her, and others, in beginning to uncover what brought their spirit joy, inspiration, comfort, and meaning.

My Spirit Board is on the previous page. I have kept it on the wall inside my closet to remind me that my soul is nourished and energized through family, community, play, photography, L'Arche, travel, nature, friendship, and by working with others towards peace and justice. When I begin to feel disconnected or down, I can look at this board and instantly be reminded to do something playful, to take my camera and go out into nature or to spend time with the people who bring me life.

Exercise: Create a Spirit Board

For this exercise, you will need the following:

Poster board or pizza round (generally pizza rounds can be found at your local craft supply store)

Old magazines and catalogs

Scissors

Glue

- Create time and space where you will not be disturbed and where you can allow your mind to wander.

- Put on some quiet music.

- Sit in a comfortable place with your magazines and catalogs.

- Simply begin to browse through them.

- Position your mind in a place of curiosity.

- As you browse, be aware of any shifts in your body as you scan the pages.

- Does an image or word catch your eye? Cut out the image or word and set it aside.

- Is there an image or word that makes you smile, take a deep breath, or fills you with awe? Cut it out and set it aside.

- When you have a number of words and pictures cut out, begin to paste them onto your board. Allow this whole process to be playful; there is no right or wrong way to do it. This is your time to get to know yourself anew, to allow yourself to be surprised, and honor those qualities, words, and pictures that create a positive, strong, and vulnerable reaction within your "Self." This is you unveiling your deep Self to yourself.

- Put your Spirit Board where you can see it often. Allow it to be a reminder that these are things that bring you joy. Make space for them. Nourish them. Tend to their unfolding.

What does your Spirit Board tell you? What is it that nourishes and energizes your whole and holy Self?

Come Home

A chorus of raindrops

Sing to me,

Come home.

Come home

Alone,

Come home.

Through the valley of loneliness

And the dark wood of fear,

Come home.

Alone,

Come home.

Leave behind your harem of expectations,

Projections,

And judgments.

Shed your mantel of loneliness,

And rinse away your fear.

For you

Alone

Belong here.

You alone

Are the one

You seek.

Once I say a complete and full "Yes"!
to a deep desire of my heart,
I wait with playful anticipation.
I keep my eyes open for
the surprising ways that the path to my dream is revealed.

Cathy and Me on Another Adventure

Manifestations Multiplied

I ALWAYS HAD A SECRET DESIRE to be on the Oprah show. I was inspired by her story, her show, and her work with young women in South Africa. As a woman who had transformed the trajectory of her life, she was a beacon for me in my own journey. Therefore, among the many items on my bucket list, three of them included: to go to the Oprah show, to be interviewed by Oprah, and to go to South Africa with Oprah. Now, in the midst of my deep grief, I said, "Yes" to the most reasonable of these three—going to the Oprah show.

As I made this decision, I did not even stop to think about how we would get tickets to the show. Luckily, my dear friend, Cathy was much more practical, and she jumped into the research. She discovered that Harpo Productions had already completed taping for the current season and would start next season's taping in September. The process of getting tickets involved watching the Oprah Show website, and on a magical day and time each month, the website would announce that the phone lines were open to get tickets to the next month's shows. The day and time the phone lines opened was different each month, and you could only get tickets for the following month's tapings.

We decided we would go to Chicago the second week in November and that we would try to get tickets for that Monday or Tuesday. We lived as if it was a done deal. On October 1, we began watching the Oprah website. Many times, each day, I checked her site to see if the phone lines were open yet. In the middle of October, we decided it was time to buy our airline tickets even though we still did not have tickets to the show.

In the third week of October, I caught the flu. Tuesday morning, feverish and miserable, I woke up and immediately checked the Oprah website. Nothing. I got Sam off to school and ran the water to take a steamy bath to break up the congestion in my lungs. Just as I was preparing to get in the tub, that quiet voice within encouraged me to check the website again. I did, and the phone lines were open! I called Cathy and my niece Michelle, who had offered to help us as a third caller and we began calling the Oprah reservation line. I skipped my bath and went back to my bed, grabbed the phone and for the next eight hours, hit redial over and over. No luck. The phone lines remained busy.

The next day, I woke up again with a fever and spent another day hitting redial. At 11:15 a.m., I got through to a recording that told me to wait for the next available agent. For thirty elated minutes I waited and then the phone line went dead! Apparently, the reservation service automatically drops calls that have been on hold for thirty minutes. In spite of my frustration and disappointment, I went back to hitting redial.

On Thursday, day three, I woke up with a low-grade fever. Another day of rest and redial. In the early afternoon, I got through to the reservation hold line. After I waited twenty-six minutes a real, live person came onto the line. I was ecstatic! Tickets were available for the Monday afternoon taping. The guest would be Russell Crowe promoting his new movie *Master and Commander*. We were invited to a private screening of the movie on Sunday evening. Although I have nothing against Russel Crowe, I had hoped for a more substantive show. I asked if there were tickets available to another show in our time frame. There was not. I gratefully accepted the tickets to see Oprah and Russell Crowe.

Now I was flying halfway across the United States to see the Oprah show. I really wanted to go to a second taping as well, but they only allow tickets for one show. I took to writing Oprah and explaining to her that coming to Chicago to see her show was a once-in-a-lifetime trip for me, and I really wanted to go to a second taping. I came up with all kinds of excuses and offers to try and meet her and to get to an additional show. She did not respond.

On my way to Chicago to see the Oprah show, I flew to Minnesota for a three-day visit with my mom. Mom was in her early eighties and had suffered many strokes. Because of the trauma to her brain, at times she acted like an angry child having a tantrum. On the second day of our visit, Mom became very angry with me for talking to my sister on the phone when she was ready to go to lunch. She shouted at me in a taunting voice, "Just go see *O*-prah! That's all you care about, *O*-prah!" It became clear that she resented that I was going to the Oprah Show. I am not sure if she was angry that I was not taking her, or if she resented that I was making another dream a reality or if she was just tired and ready for me to leave. I spent the evening working through my anger and resentment, determined to end our time on a positive note and committed to enjoy my time in Chicago without guilt.

The next morning, Cathy and I boarded our plane, excited for the adventure ahead and for this time away together. We arrived in Chicago, checked into our room, wandered around the Navy pier, and headed to a private screening of *Master and Commander*. At the theater, the Oprah team welcomed us with free popcorn and drinks. We watched the show and then headed back to our hotel.

In the morning, we were at the Oprah studios nice and early to secure our place in line. We waited outside for a couple hours before they opened the doors. Once inside we waited to go into the studio. Finally, we were in our seats. I was in a chair that bordered the walkway where Oprah would be entering. I was so excited to see this iconic woman. Her power, clarity, and drive to make a positive difference with her show and with her life were an inspiration to me. Oprah walked into the studio and my eyes filled with tears. As she walked past me, she made eye contact and quickly shook my hand. I drank it all in. I do not remember much about her interview with Russell Crowe. I do remember what it felt like to be in the presence of this powerful woman, who had made her own deep dreams come true. It felt hopeful.

After the show, one of the producers announced that they were looking for audience members for the next day's show. She asked if there were people in the audience who had preteen children and would be willing to come back the next day, to please come and talk to her. Cathy had four preteen children. I grabbed her arm and said, "Let's go!"

The producer interviewed Cathy for about twenty minutes, asking her questions about her children and about leaving them home alone. Then she turned to me and asked, "How about you? Do you have children?"

I replied, "I have a five-year-old, but I do not leave him home alone. However, I was left home alone as a young child. By the time I was eight, I was babysitting a two-year-old and a newborn late into the evenings, thirty minutes from my home."

This caught the producer's attention, and she began to ask me questions about my experience. At one point she asked, "If you could go back and change your childhood, would you?"

I thought for a moment and replied, "I do not know who I would be without those experiences. Some of my greatest gifts were born out of being an overly responsible child. So, I guess my answer is no."

"Can you give us an example of a gift you acquired from those experiences?"

I replied, "When I was around eight years old, I was home babysitting my little sister. My mom was raising us all on her own by then, and she and my older siblings were at work. She had left me a list of chores to accomplish that day. I remember calling over my neighborhood friends and saying, 'Let's play house!' The next thing I knew, one child was vacuuming, another one was dusting, and someone was cleaning off the counters. I was standing at the sink doing dishes when I thought, 'This is how you do it!' That was the day my delegation skills were born."

She asked, "Why don't you leave your son home alone?"

I explained, "Because I do not need to. My mom was a single mom with eight children. My dad was living on the streets, and my mom had to work to support us. I have a husband, and we have a community around us that we can call at any time for help with our son and they would be there to help us. My mom did not have that luxury."

The producer asked us, "If we need you to come back tomorrow and be part of our audience, would you be able to attend the show?"

"What time would you need us?" I asked.

"We would need you here by noon."

"OK. We have tickets to the Manet exhibit at the Art Institute of Chicago at ten. We will just go to the exhibit and not tour the rest of the museum, so that we can be here on time."

"Great! I'll call you if we need you."

Cathy and I headed out for lunch. During lunch, Cathy's phone rang. It was the producer, inviting us to attend the next day's taping. My goal of going to a second show was fulfilled. I was bubbling with excitement!

Later that night, we were in our hotel room visiting, when Cathy's cell phone rang. She answered and I heard her saying, "Yes...OK...Ah-huh... Sure...OK!" She got off the phone and with her eyes twinkling and a giggle bubbling out, she turned to me and said, "That was the producer from the Oprah Show. They wondered if they could send a car to pick us up at the Art Institute tomorrow. They want to interview you on the air!"

I was excited, terrified, amazed, and overwhelmed. What was I going to wear? What was I going to say? How was I going to answer Oprah's questions without offending my mom or the rest of my family? My mom was already resentful of me going to the Oprah show. I did not want to say anything that would make her feel any shame. I was up most of the night, too anxious to sleep.

We got up in the morning and got ready for the big day—first the Manet exhibit and then on to the Oprah show. My stomach was full of knots, and I could not eat breakfast. Cathy and I toured the Manet exhibit and as we exited the museum, there was a limousine parked out front, with a beautiful black man in a dark suit standing outside. Timidly, we walked towards the car. He called out, "Kim Ebert?" I put my hand up and waved and said, "That's me." Cathy and I giggled like young school girls as he opened our car door.

He drove to the back entrance of the Oprah studios and ushered us out of the car. We were met at the door by a young woman who took Cathy directly into the studio and seated her. The producer took me into the green room, where they did my hair and makeup and where there were all sorts of snacks and drinks available. Once I was ready, the producer went through the script. She told me that I would be sitting in one of the first two rows. When I was introduced, I was to stand and Oprah would ask me a few questions. They really wanted me to emphasize my previous comments about why I would not leave my son alone and my reflection on the support systems I had in place that would not make it necessary to leave him home alone. It all seemed easy enough.

When Oprah introduced me and I stood up to talk with her, she did not start with the question they had shown me. Instead, she asked, "Who were these children that you were babysitting when you were just eight years old?" I froze. I was not prepared for this question and had not thought through how to answer it without offending my family. They were the children of a family member. I could hear the criticisms I would encounter if I talked about this on national TV. I stammered, "They were children that I was paid to babysit." From that moment on, I lost all focus and the words I had so authentically spoken the day before were lost to me. Oprah tried a few different ways to get me to focus on why I would not leave my son home alone, but I just kept saying, "No. I would never leave him home alone." I never spoke to why I would not need to leave him alone or the support systems we had in place. I knew I had choked. The Oprah staff was very gracious. And I was able to hold onto my excitement of having fulfilled my dream as the chauffeur drove us back to our hotel in the limousine.

———————— ◗◆◖ ————————

Weeks later, I got a phone call from the Oprah producer, giving me the date and time that my show would air. I was excited and nervous. How would my family react to the show? I had prayed that the show would not hurt or shame them in any way. The day of the show, I made popcorn, then Niko, Sam, and I snuggled in to watch the show. Things progressed as I had experienced them. I saw myself sitting in the second row as Oprah took the stage. Oprah introduced the topic and she interviewed one person after another. As the woman she had interviewed before me spoke, my anxiety grew. I was next. She finished talking to that woman and went to commercial. I was next! When the show returned, the next interviewee was a woman who spoke after me. Wait, what?!!!! They cut me out! They. Cut. Me. Out. I was astonished and then I laughed and laughed. I got to go to the Oprah show. I was interviewed by Oprah and got the whole experience of the green room, having my hair and makeup done, experiencing what it's like behind the scenes, AND I did not offend my family!

Love calls us to go beyond our fears and discomfort.
It calls us to surrender to our deep spirit and
To allow that spirit to guide us.

Ocean City, Washington, 2012

Empower the Authentic Self

LIFE PRESENTS EACH OF US WITH opportunities to go beyond our comfort zone, to stand in our power and to embody our gifts in new and unexpected ways. Niko's mom, Jerry, invited me to go to the appointment with her oncologist where she would be receiving the results of her tests. We already knew that she had endometrial cancer. This meeting would give us her prognosis and treatment plan. I knew that as much as I loved my mother-in-law, I would be the least affected family member in the room. It would be my job to hold the energy for Niko, his sisters, and his dad. I would need to listen deeply, ask clarifying questions, and record all the doctor had to say. I would need to stay as clear, focused, and objective as possible.

When my friend, Bob died, Sam was only four years old. It was his first encounter with death. How we navigated this unexpected death would color Sam's future relationship to death. In the midst of my own grief, I needed to stay calm and authentic while acting as a teacher, guide, and mom for Sam.

When Pennye asked me to preside at Etta's funeral, I was terrified and humbled. I had never presided over a funeral before. Over six hundred people would be attending. I needed to bathe myself in compassion so that I could meet their deep grief and guide them through a celebration of Etta's life.

And when Cathy told me that they wanted to interview me on the Oprah show, even though I had fantasized about it, the reality shook me to my core.

In each of these big events, I was being called to go beyond myself and to take on a role that I was not expecting. I could have said no to Jerry and Pennye. I could have turned around and walked out of the facility when Bob died. Love calls us to go beyond our fears and discomfort. It calls us to surrender to our deep spirit and to allow that spirit to guide us.

We will not always do this perfectly. At times, fear will overtake us, as it did in me on the Oprah show. I allowed fear to take over and I lost touch with my core. These moments of fear are great teachers. They remind us how important it is to stay connected to our most authentic Self. I can look back on that moment when Oprah asked, "Who were these children that you were babysitting at the age of eight?" My response could have been, "They were the children of a family member." With such a large family, no one would have known if that meant a sibling, or an aunt, uncle or cousin. If I had answered in this way, my field would not have become contracted with fear and worry would not have replaced my authenticity.

When I am faced with a difficult or powerful task, I illuminate my field. This allows me to connect to a power greater than myself and to allow that power to penetrate every cell of my being. It empowers me, guides me, and grounds me into the deepest, most authentic, and powerful aspects of myself.

Exercise: Illuminate Your Field

When I illuminate my field, I use the images of the Divine that are familiar and nurturing to me. I imagine a ball of Christ energy or a ball of Universal Love.

Use an image that fills you with Love, Peace and Clarity, an image that expands your awareness and that brings you home to your truest, most vital, and most brilliant self.

- You can do this exercise sitting, standing or lying down.

- Close your eyes.

- Take a few deep breaths all the way down into your belly.

- Imagine a golden ball a few feet above your head.

- Bring your awareness up into that ball of light.

- Now let that light flow into you, lighting up each atom of your being with love.

- Feel this light flow in you, around you, and through you, until each and every atom of your being is filled, held, and bathed in love.

- In this place, ask for any guidance and direction that you need for the day or the task at hand.

As you bring yourself back into the world, take this sense of calm, clarity, and light with you. As you go through your day, when you feel yourself curling into isolation or contracting into impatience, fear, or negativity, close your eyes for just a moment and reconnect to that ball of light. Let it fill you, guide you, and strengthen you. Follow where it leads and allow your brilliance to radiate into the world.

Don't Be Afraid

Dear One,

Don't be afraid.

Come!

Curl into the lap of my love.

Feel yourself cradled in compassion.

Hear the lullabies of longing for your spirit

To be released into the world.

You have stood silent too long.

It is time to stand in your truth

And speak clear and strong.

No need for anger or righteousness.

No need to be "Right"

Or to prove anyone "Wrong."

Speak with clarity and courage.

Listen with an open heart.

When you slip back into old patterns,

Recognize it and shift.

Do not wait until you can do it perfectly.

Do it as well as you can each day, in each moment.

When you fail,

Discover the lesson.

Then start anew and

Try again.

I am light.
I am loved.
I am worthy.
I Am.

South Africa, 2004

Say Yes Again

I DID NOT GO TO SOUTH Africa with Oprah, but because of my time at the Oprah show, I went to South Africa.

After the taping of the second show, the limo took us back to our hotel. I packed up my bags to return to Tacoma. Cathy's husband, Dave, had arrived and he and Cathy were staying in Chicago for a few days. We met up with him in the hotel bar. Dave was having a martini. Never having had a martini, I thought I would try one as we told him about the adventures of our day. On my empty stomach, I felt tipsy after only a few sips. I handed my martini to Dave and started drinking water. Thirty minutes later, I left Cathy and Dave and headed to the airport. Still feeling the effects of the alcohol, I slept on the plane until we reached the Minneapolis airport, where I had a two-hour layover before boarding for Tacoma.

When I got off the plane in Minneapolis, I knew I needed to get some food into my body. Touring the food court, I saw a California Pizza Oven. I thought to myself, "What the heck is a California pizza?" I would have jumped at a chance for a Minnesota pizza. The greasiest, cheesiest, and most delicious pizza I have ever had comes from Minnesota.

I noticed a woman eating a broccoli pizza and knew that only in California would you find a pizza with broccoli. I walked up to the woman and asked, "Is that any good?"

"It is quite good," she replied. "Would you like to join me?"

Startled and afraid that she thought I was asking for a handout, I replied, "No. I can buy my own food."

As I started to walk away, she said, "There is no way that I can eat all of this. If you don't help me, I will have to throw it away."

Her kind eyes and warm spirit broke through my defenses. I took a deep breath and sat down with this stranger to share her pizza. We introduced ourselves, and I was surprised to discover that she, too, was from Western Washington. She was on her way home from New York City where she had been at a board meeting for an international program that I deeply respect. As we continued to talk about her work, she proclaimed, "My real passion is taking women to South Africa to immerse them in the AIDS pandemic." She went on to explain that every year she took a delegation of women from the United States to South Africa to witness the plight of women and families within the AIDS pandemic. They visited hospice programs, hospitals, clinics, orphanages, and feeding programs. The purpose of the trip was to raise the participants' consciousness so that they would come back to the United States as spokespeople for these vulnerable members of our human family. As she described the experience, I found my mouth declare with conviction, "I could find ten women to do that!"

My mind was sputtering, "What are you talking about??? Where will you get the money? What about Sam, how will he get to preschool each day? Who will take care of him in the afternoon before Niko gets home? Who are these nine other women you think you can find to go on this journey?" Despite these thoughts, my mouth continued talking as if my rational mind did not even exist.

I took time to sit with the various voices in me. The more I sat with the voice that said, "Do this," the more energy and excitement I felt growing in me and the quieter the voice of doubt became. I talked it over with Niko and Sam and with their support, I said "Yes" to what I had instinctively known all along: I was called to go on this journey.

With my fully committed "Yes," things started to happen.

I participated in a conference call about the trip. Afterwards, I called Cathy and told her about my experiences in the Minneapolis airport.

After I had finished, she said, "You're going to South Africa, aren't you?"

"Yes, and I think you should go with me."

Cathy laughed and said, "You know I live vicariously through you on these adventures."

"I think this time you need to join me."

A week later, Cathy called me back. She was going to South Africa! Pennye decided to join us. Then two other friends joined our small group.

My friend, Marcia, was undecided. Before Mass one Sunday, she told me she was eighty percent sure that she would be going. Throughout the Mass, I was distracted by my six-year-old son and his gaggle of friends who sat in the pew with me. My attention was brought back to the Service during Communion when the choir began to sing a chant to the rhythm of a drum. The first two verses were in a language I did not recognize and then the congregation joined in as they were repeated in English. *Send me. Send me. Send me, Lord. Send me. Send me. Send me. I will go. I will go. I will go, Lord. I will go. I will go. I will go.* As I sang and swayed to the beat of the drum, Niko tapped me on the arm and pointed to the song sheet. This was a South African hymn!

After Mass, Marcia and I hugged as she told me she was going with me. What other sign could she need? I did not find ten women, but I was excited and amazed that five women I loved and respected were headed to South Africa with me!

Everything I needed was provided. I wrote a letter to share my plans with friends and family. I invited them to join me on this journey by praying for me and/or sponsoring me. The support poured in.

A woman who was speaking at the Evangelical Lutheran Women's Conference closed her talk with my fundraising letter and asked the attendees to support this project.

People collected bed protectors, basic medical supplies, sheets, Beanie Babies, crayons, scarves, and jewelry that we were able to pack in our suitcases to distribute to the organizations and individuals we would meet.

At that time, it was unusual for the poor in South Africa to have pictures of themselves. So, I bought a Polaroid camera to take pictures of the people we would meet that I could leave with them. I wrote Polaroid and asked them to donate film. When I did not hear back from them, I decided to elicit help from Ellen DeGeneres, in the hope that her celebrity could assist me in getting the film from Polaroid. I wrote to her through her website and told her about the trip I was taking to South Africa to study and witness the AIDS pandemic, and about my desire to be able to take photos that I could leave with the people. I asked her to call Polaroid and to ask them to donate film. Four days later, Polaroid contacted me saying that it looked like they were going to give me film. I wrote to Ellen to give her the news. If she had called, I wanted to say thank you; if she hadn't called, I wanted her to know that I would not need her help after all. Two weeks later, I received a letter from Polaroid saying that they could not give me any film. I immediately contacted Ellen via her website and shared with her that I had just received a rejection letter from Polaroid. Again, I told her why I thought this film was important. Twelve hours later, I got a phone call from Polaroid. They were sending me enough film for five hundred and ninety pictures! Excitedly, I sent Ellen a thank-you letter. I do not know if Ellen called Polaroid or not. I never received any correspondence from her. All I know is that every time I contacted her about getting film, I received a direct response from Polaroid.

By the time I left for South Africa, I had not only received the money I needed for my direct expenses, but also over $3,000 in additional donations. I left knowing that I was carrying the love and care of each person who had donated. I was going to South Africa to represent each of these people. At the end of our time in South Africa, I sat with Cathy and Marcia and together we chose how we would disperse the donations I had received. I was honored to deliver the funds, in the name of all those who had supported this journey, to the South African organizations and programs that had most impressed us.

"We are here to support and guide you.
Love is made manifest as you step onto your path.
Do not tremble. Do not be afraid, for you do not walk alone.
We walk with you."

I Am
South Africa, 2004

Soul Council

SOUL WORK REQUIRES THAT I TAKE time alone, in quiet, to listen to the whisperings of my spirit. However, once I have given my full "Yes" and am ready to act on the urgings of my spirit, I create a circle of support around me. In the case of going to South Africa, I asked for the support and blessings of my beloveds, Niko and Sam. I reached out to my community of friends and asked for their support. The Sunday before we left, our parish community prayed a blessing over us. When we were in South Africa, I asked two of my dear friends who were there with me to help me make the important decisions of how to distribute the additional money that was donated. These circles of support amplified my "Yes" to the project or dream. They provided energy, wise counsel, resources, and accountability.

I also requested help from the spiritual realm: angels, ancestors, and holy men and women. I asked for angels of protection, love, compassion, and humility to surround me. I asked the spirit of my grandma Rose to travel with me. I asked Jesus, Mother Mary, and Mother Teresa to guide me. Embraced by this extraordinary network, I left on this adventure. I felt surrounded, guided, and supported. I knew I was not alone.

When I have a big decision to make and I need guidance, I sit with my Soul Council. This is a meditative process. I wait for a time when the house is totally quiet, and I know I will not be disturbed. I take time to center myself by breathing deeply for a few minutes. Then I ask for a number of how many will be attending and I put out a seat for each of my council members. I write down the name of each person who shows up. Some of the attendees are those whose spirit I have specifically asked to join the group; others just show up. I allow this to be a playful process and I let my imagination take the helm.

When the circle is complete, I ask this council to guide me. I listen to each of them one by one and write down their responses. I do not edit what they say to fit my assumptions. I just let the information flow.

In one such Soul Council, the following members were in attendance:

Me

Mary Magdalene

Sekhmet, Egyptian warrior goddess

Princess Diana—this was the attendee that surprised me the most. Although I respect her, I have no specific affinity towards her.

Jesus

My Guardian Angel

Archangel Michael

Alethea, Speaker of Truth

As the meeting began, I heard them say, "There are seven of us here. We are here to support and guide you. Love is made manifest as you step onto your path. Do not tremble. Do not be afraid, for you do not walk alone. We walk with you."

Here is a transcript from part of our meeting:

"Kim, get out of your head. You are limiting too much…We need you travelling, teaching, and writing."

Kim: "Do I really need to travel, teach, and write?"

Jesus: "Yes, my dear one, you do. I need you to spread my word of love, gratitude, and compassion. I need you to help others to see that I live in each cell of their being, that they are worthy of their own love. There is an incredible journey waiting just for them within their very selves."

Mary Magdalene: "Kim, I am with you. I will go with you into those places you do not feel prepared to go. I will help you face those who criticize, condemn, frighten, or threaten your very core. Do not fear. I will be there."

Sekhmet: "There is great knowledge that has been given to you. Set your fear aside and share it."

Alethea: "You know you have to speak it, Girl. Speak it. Write it. Live it!"

Angel Michael: "I am here to help you cut the cords to all that holds you back and to help you clear the pathway to your life's dream. I've got your back."

Princess Diana: "I will remind you of your softness. Together we will serve the poorest of the poor. We will bring hope and beauty and grace."

Guardian Angel: "I am here with you always. I will bring you the support you need if you only ask."

Kim: "What are my next steps?"

Council: "Take a bath."

"Ground your energy."

"Commit to this committee."

"Stay in quiet. No TV or games."

"Write today."

"Pray...Listen...Keep your pen and journal handy."

"Bring each of us to the party with you."

"Never go alone."

Exercise: Create a Soul Council

Who are the people in your life who you seek out for wisdom and counsel?

Which ancestors, saints, angels or deities do you turn to for support?

Which of them would you invite to be on your soul council?

Who would show up unexpectedly to join your council?

What questions would you ask?

Take some time now to explore these questions and to write down the answers. When the time comes, when you need the extra support, direction, wisdom, or courage, call on those people in your life who you can lean on and take the time to convene your Soul Council and discover the direction, wisdom, and courage they offer.

I Am

I Am.
I am one
With the Great I Am.
I am light.
I am loved.
I am worthy.
I Am.

I see
The faces
Of the ancestors
Etched in nature.
In cliffs, trees,
And waterfalls,
I see them.

I am surrounded
By the power of
Their endless support.
And I know I am
Encouraged,
Protected and
Loved.

Joy streamed out of her.
Love for herself and
For her own beauty overflowed.

Mary, 2010

And Again

As a result of my experiences in South Africa, I was invited to be on the board for The Lesotho Connection (TLC). This non-profit organization was created to support the vulnerable and orphaned children of Lesotho, a very small country encircled by South Africa, known as the mountain kingdom.

One evening, at our TLC board meeting, a letter was read from the director of our local L'Arche community. A new assistant named Mary was joining the community for one year. She was from Lesotho. They were looking for a host family. I was very excited and committed to talking it over with Niko and Sam. I went home and presented this proposal to them, and as a family we agreed to welcome Mary into our home and lives.

In August of 2009, Mary entered our home and moved into our hearts. She immediately called me Mommy; Niko, Daddy; and Sam, her brother. She was so excited to meet all of us, most especially her brother, Sam. Over the years, we have had other students from other countries live with us, but this was different. Mary entered our family completely and filled a space in each of us. She is the daughter of my heart who enjoys talking with me late into the night, who looks to me for wisdom and advice, who cheers me on, and who affirms my strength, beauty, and goodness with gusto. She is Sam's biggest cheerleader. She thinks her brother is the smartest and most talented young man on the planet. Her love for him is unconditional and full-hearted. She is Niko's best audience. Niko loves his own jokes and often gets an eye roll from Sam and me when we hear the same joke again and again. Mary hears each joke as if it is for the first time and laughs and laughs with her dad. When I was in South Africa in 2004, I was amazed by the strength, beauty, and joy of the women we met. Mary embodies these same qualities. Her free expression of delight and joy have been a gift to each of us.

———————◦◆◦———————

One day in December, Mary taught me an important lesson on delight. She came into my office clutching a pink hat to her chest. Her dark eyes were smiling as she asked, "Is this for me?"

"Where did you find it?" I replied.

"Under my pillow."

"It must be from the Advent Fairy," I said. The Advent Fairy is a tradition we started when Sam was a small child. Every night of Advent—the four weeks leading up to Christmas—the Advent Fairy brings a small gift.

Stretching out her arms, cradling the pink hat in her hands, and with her face radiant with joy, Mary exclaimed, "I think I like this!"

Standing before the mirror in the bathroom, Mary put on her new hat. Turning herself this way and then that way, hands framing her face, Mary admired herself in her new pink hat.

"I am a pretty lady...I love myself in my new hat...I am so beautiful... Oh, I like myself in this hat!"

On and on she went. Joy streamed out of her, love for herself and her own beauty overflowed. Mary admired herself in the mirror for many minutes. Several times, throughout the day, she went back to the mirror to sneak another peak of herself in her new hat.

I watched in awe and wondered, "How did I lose the ability to fully appreciate and love myself in my own body?" I had never witnessed another woman admire and delight in her physical being before.

A prayer whispered in my heart, "May we all sneak a peek in our mirrors and, without criticism or shame, may we express our delight and joy in our own reflection."

You are an original.
Look at the seeming imperfections of your body and
begin to see them as originalities, medals, and
a roadmap of the life you have lived.
You are a masterpiece!

La Push, Washington, 1989

Coming Home to a Body I Love

"How did I lose the ability to fully appreciate and love myself in my own body?" I knew the answer to this question had its roots in my childhood. The comment that "I was so ugly that I stunk" was proclaimed on a regular basis by one of my siblings who was afraid I would become conceited if they did not help me to think less of myself. It worked. I came to believe that I was not as beautiful or pretty or as worthy as others and that any appreciation of my own beauty or goodness, in itself, made me ugly. After watching Mary appreciate herself in her new pink hat, I knew that it was time for me to release all residual noise within me from that old lie. It was essential now, as a woman, to reclaim my delight in my reflection, in my "Self" in this body.

The name of my business is Body Sacred. For over thirty years, my mission has been to assist women in reclaiming the sacred dimension of their own physical being. My focus has been on assisting others in learning to come home to their bodies: to recognize that each cell of their being is holy and has a specific purpose to fulfill; to explore and respond lovingly to the messages their body gives them; to be a loving steward of their body rather than a harsh taskmaster; and, to stand in awe of the amazing miracles that are performed each and every moment in their own physical being.

I am an agent of change for women's relationship with their bodies, but I realized I had missed an important piece. I was working to assist women in coming home to their bodies and to respect and love their physical form, but to delight in their own beauty? To radiate joy at their reflection in the mirror? This was new territory for me.

I knew that I was at an important edge in my own growth and healing. I started with small steps. I changed the recorded messages on my electronics to say "Hi, Beautiful!" I took time to smile at my reflection in the mirror, to just stand there and to smile at myself and to whisper "I am Good. I am Beautiful. I am Holy." I released judgment of my physical form and began to enjoy myself as I am: my short stature, big bones, large feet, round soft belly, white hair, and wisdom lines around my eyes. I began to buy a couple pieces of clothing each season that I loved to wear, and when I wore them, I found myself standing taller and walking more confidently. I made them the core pieces of my wardrobe. It did not matter if anyone else loved them. It mattered that I loved wearing them and that when I looked in the mirror, I loved what I saw. I purged clothing that I did not love or that did not raise my vibrancy when I wore them.

How did I know if a piece of clothing increased my vibrancy? I did not need to ask myself, should I keep this piece? Do I love it? If I found myself asking those questions, I let it go. I only kept the clothes that I loved wearing. Ugly underwear…gone. Bras that poked or pinched… gone. Sentimental pieces that no longer served me…gone. Pants that I could not move freely in or felt tight or just didn't fit quite right…gone. Shirts and dresses that I never wore anymore…gone.

As I became more discerning about how I felt in the clothes I wore, I began to buy fewer items that were "a good deal." Rather, I limited my purchases to ones that allowed me to feel good, look good, and move with more confidence and joy in the world. I began to notice that I was smiling at myself more freely in the mirror. With delight, I heard myself saying, "Oh, I love myself in this! I look beautiful!" I had not only come home to my body, I was home in a body I loved.

Exercise: Celebrate Your Beauty

Can you look in the mirror and enjoy who and what you see? If so, congratulations! You have let go of, or never took on, the cultural norms of perfection. That is awesome!

Remove Judgment

If you cannot look in the mirror and enjoy what you see, what gets in the way? Is it shame? Judgment? Both? Create rituals to quiet the inner critic. Remember the mantra you created in the RELEASE section to shift your beliefs? Did your mantra include an affirmation of your beauty? If not, go back and rework your mantra or create a new mantra that includes "I am beautiful." Say this mantra every time you look in the mirror or any time you start to criticize your physical self in any way.

Find Beauty in Each Seeming Imperfection

Each of us is an original work of art. Some of us don't follow the mass-market stereotype of beauty, but that does not make us any less beautiful. You are an original. Look at the seeming imperfections of your body and begin to see them as originalities, medals, and a roadmap of the life you have lived. You are a masterpiece!

Remind Yourself That You Are Beautiful

Put a note on your mirror that says "Hi, Beautiful!" Program your electronics to call you "Beautiful" instead of your name.

Look at Yourself in the Mirror Each Day

Look at yourself in the mirror every day and say, "You are beautiful." If you cannot look at your whole face then start by looking only at your eyes. Do you find yourself criticizing your eyes? Then look just at the pupil or find one spot on your face that you can look at, love, and say, "Hello, Beautiful!" and mean it. Say this to yourself every day. Gradually take in more and more of your face, until you can smile at your reflection and appreciate your unique beauty.

Purge Anything That Makes You Feel Less Than the Incredible Work of Art You Are

Purge your closets and drawers of all clothing and accessories that you do not love, need, or wear. Keep it simple. Do you love the color? Do you love how it feels? Do you love how you feel in it? Does it bring you delight? Is it free of stains and rips? Is it in working order? Are all the buttons there? Does the zipper work? If you said no to any of these questions and it is not an item you absolutely need, such as a work uniform or medical stockings, get rid of it.

Examine Your Self Talk

Take note of how much time you spend each day criticizing or shaming yourself. How much energy do you invest in making yourself small or invisible? As you let go of judgment, your inner critic will take a back seat, making room for love and appreciation to come forward. Welcome them. When the inner critic is not our primary personal resource, there is much less drama in our inner dialogue and much less chatter. The voices of love and appreciation do not suppress our energy, rather they expand it and increase our vitality. This frees up space for the energies of clarity and direction to come forward with more ease.

The Truth of My I Am

Tears surface
As sadness rumbles in my core.
Feelings of unworthiness
Crumble,
Leaving me standing
In fear
Of my own goodness,
My own beauty,
My own Holy Self.
I am worthy
Quietly echoes in my soul.
I am worthy.

Terrified to take this in,
To stand
In the truth of my
I Am,
I breath deeply,
I stand tall,
And my tears of triumph
Flow.

❋ *Tend*

When you bring forth a deep dream,

Do not set it aside like a trophy,

Or resist its presence

So that you can stay in the familiar field of longing.

Open your heart,

Your mind,

Your soul,

And receive it.

Your deep dream has arrived.

I was moved by this man's tender spirit.
I watched him dance freely and playfully.
He treated each person with humility, respect and delight.

Niko, 2002

A Safe Home for My Spirit

HOME, HUSBAND, CHILDREN—THESE WERE THE DEEP yearnings of my soul. I had my first boyfriend when I was ten. One of my aunts did not want her daughter to spend too much time with me because she considered me "boy crazy." I wasn't boy crazy; I was just crazy for one boy, a boy I had a crush on since second grade. Our courtship was innocent enough. He walked me home after school, and we sat on the curb a block away from home and talked about our future with ten—yes, ten—children. We never kissed or even hugged; we just walked home together and planned the future of our dreams.

From the time I was thirteen, I consistently had a boyfriend. Some were fleeting, but many were long-term relationships that lasted up to five years. More than one of these beaus asked me to marry him. I held back. When I left for the Pacific Northwest in 1984 to join the Jesuit Volunteer Corps, I remember telling my longtime boyfriend, "I feel like I need to choose between you and God."

"Why do you need to choose?" He asked with confusion.

"I don't know; I just know I can't have both."

Now I understand that I intuitively knew I could not follow my spirit and be in a relationship with him. I instinctively knew I would compromise my core, and I would slowly, yet steadily, become smaller. Also, my boyfriend could not pass the questions of my heart: Could I trust him with my spirit? Would he be the kind of father that I wanted for the child I knew I would have one day? I could not confidently say "Yes" to both of these questions and so I knew this relationship would not last.

My dating dance for much of my young adult years followed a pattern of two steps forward, one step back. I would risk dating someone I respected and liked, and when the relationship ended, I would move on to someone I liked but would never trust with my heart or my future. I felt comfortable with these men I did not trust. They were familiar, they fit in with my family, and my mom adored each one. I clung to the familiar. We would break up, and I would begin dating other men, men out of my comfort zone. When those relationships did not work out, back to the familiar I would go.

When I was thirty-three, the last of these familiar relationships ended, and so did my dance. I was ready to let go, to move out of my comfort zone and find a life partner that I loved, trusted, and respected and with whom I would trust having a child. It had taken time, lots of therapy, self-exploration, and healing. I was finally ready and finally believed that I was worthy of the kind of relationship my soul had been urging me towards.

To cultivate the ground of this new kind of relationship, I cut ties with men that were hanging out in my field. I knew that if I was really ready for a lasting relationship, I needed to make space within me and release attachments to men I could run back to if things did not work out. I needed to stand alone in my desire for a life partner. I needed to stand in my vulnerability and to step boldly towards my dream.

I made a list of essential characteristics that I would not compromise in a life partner. My partner needed to be gentle, strong, honest, faithful, loyal, intelligent, conscious, fun, spiritual, loving, committed to his own growth, and open to marriage and children.

Then I made a commitment to myself: the moment I realized that any man I was dating did not have these essential qualities, our courtship was over. This list made dating much more fun. I did not need to pursue a relationship with someone just because we both had a mutual attraction. I could say, "No thank you," and move on! The boundaries this list created felt incredibly freeing, empowering, and drama-free.

In May of 1993, just five months after I made my list, I went to a dance to benefit the Seattle L'Arche community with my friend Adrian. Late into the evening, I saw a man enter the hall. He was tall and thin with a short beard. He was wearing a trench coat and had long, curly hair tied in a ponytail. I thought to myself, "That man looks interesting, a bit scruffy, but interesting." I bought myself a beer, sat down, and studied him for the next thirty minutes. I was moved by this man's beautiful and tender spirit. I watched him dance freely and playfully. His eyes twinkled as he sought out and danced with different core members. He treated each person, with or without disability, with humility, respect, and delight. I turned to Adrian, and said, "I want a date with that man by the end of the night."

Ten minutes later, my friend Tara arrived. This scruffy, beautiful man walked right over to her and gave her a big hug. Here was my opening! As soon as he danced himself away from her, I walked up to Tara and asked, "Who was that man?"

She replied, "Oh, that's Niko. He's a god. He works with Kevin in detention ministry." (Kevin is Tara's husband, and the friend I have known the longest in the Pacific Northwest.)

I said, "I highly doubt that he's a god, but I would like to meet him."

Tara squealed with delight and started dancing towards Niko. I felt vulnerable and exposed so I headed to the bathroom, telling her I would be back in a moment. When I returned, Tara and Niko were visiting as they danced. I sashayed over and joined in. Tara introduced me and then pranced away, leaving Niko and me dancing together. The song ended and a slow song began.

Niko looked down at me and asked, "Would you like to slow dance with me?"

With unknown boldness, I replied, "I would love to slow dance with you!"

As we danced, we began to talk and learn about each other.

I discovered that he had taken a year off and travelled by bus from Spokane, Washington, through Mexico and into Central America by himself. I had taken three months off and travelled to Thailand, Nepal, and India by myself. He had been a youth minister for four years. I had been a youth minister for five years. He had graduated with a Master's degree from Seattle University's School of Theology and Ministry. I was working on my Master's degree from the same program. I asked him what he had done for his completion project.

He replied, "I took a group of high school students down to the barrios of Tijuana, in 1989, to work in a program called Los Niños."

With astonishment I said, "Oh, I took a group of students down to the barrios of Tijuana to work in Los Niños in 1989! When were you there?"

He had been there in August, and I had been there in April.

The clincher was that he was receiving a massage once a month for his self-care. This told me that he, like myself, valued his body and cared about nourishing himself and maintaining balance in his life.

At the end of that slow song, the event came to an end. Breathing into my boldness, I looked at him and said, "Well, Niko, I would like to continue this conversation sometime, if you are up for that."

He responded, "I don't have any paper or pen to give you my number."

"Well, Kevin and Tara must have your number. I will get it from them."

"No, I will go find something," he stammered.

Moments later, I saw him sitting in the furthest corner in the hall writing on a piece of paper. When he returned, he handed me his number.

With another breath of boldness, I said, "Well, Niko, I will be in Seattle the next three Mondays. Is there a Monday that would work best for you?"

"This Monday would work."

"Great! Where shall we meet?"

I was astounded by my clarity and persistence. But I knew! I knew this person was someone special and I did not want to miss the opportunity to know him. Later that night, I wrote in my journal:

Dear Niko,

Are you who you seem to be? Are you gentle, strong, committed, searching, deep, intelligent, sensual, interested, conscious, fun, intense, sincere, and honest?

Twenty-five years later, I can honestly say, "He is all that and more."

*Ask the Archangel Michael to come with his luminous sword and
cut all the cords that no longer serve you, others, or the world.*

Lily, 2005

Space for Something New

IN ORDER TO HAVE ROOM IN my life for a lifetime partner, it was imperative that I make space within myself. Releasing my ties to the "just-in-case-men" allowed me to create that space for someone new to come forward. I have found the following exercise very helpful as I continue to follow my spirit and dare to call myself forward into the most authentic and true version of myself and my relationships.

For years, I had stomach pains in the middle of my stomach right below my sternum. This is also the location of the third chakra—the power chakra—and mine was out of balance. I saw many doctors and had many tests to no avail. A friend told me about Allison Scott, a South African healer, who was visiting our city and available to give treatments. I made an appointment with her. During our session, Allison led me through a process of cutting cords. In less than an hour, I had cut the cords in over ten relationships and my stomach pain was significantly reduced.

The concept of cutting cords does not mean that I cut the connection to that person. Rather, it means that I cut the cords between us that no longer serve me, them, or the world. I use this exercise to cut cords with out-of-date parts of myself, with my core relationships, with clients, and with anyone who happens to be taking up real estate in my mind. This exercise is especially important in my relationship with Niko and my relationship with our son, Sam. If I am relating to Niko or parenting Sam from the same place we were a year ago, then I am out of date and cannot be the kind of partner or parent they need now. I want to keep my relationships current. Releasing old, out-of-date cords, helps me do that.

Exercise: Cut Old Cords

- Sit in a comfortable chair with your feet on the floor.

- Take a few deep breaths to calm and center yourself.

- As you breathe, imagine yourself and the person you need to cut cords with standing, facing one another.

- See the cords flowing between your solar plexus to theirs. The old, out-of-date cords look dull, ugly and grey and they are pulsating.

- Ask the Archangel Michael to come with his luminous blue sword and cut all the cords that no longer serve you, the other, or the world. Archangel Michael is believed to be a leader in the angelic realm who assists us when we need protection, who helps us release fear, doubt, and confusion, and supports us in moving forward in our life.

- Imagine Archangel Michael standing on your right between the two of you.

- See him raise his luminous blue sword and in one swift movement bring it down, and as he slices through these old cords, they transform into light and disappear.

- All that remains are the positive and life-giving cords between you. They may be white or golden, and they feel vibrant and alive.

- Looking deeply into this person's eyes with tenderness, tell them, "I love you, and I am sorry for any and all ways that I have hurt or offended you. I forgive myself, and I ask you to please forgive me."

- Wait patiently until they forgive you.

- See them look at you and hear them say, "I love you, and I am sorry for any ways that I have hurt or offended you. Please forgive me."

- When you are ready, tell them that you forgive them. ("I forgive you" does not mean what you did is OK. It means, "I am no longer willing to carry the pain of your actions.")

- Feel yourselves embrace each other.

- As you let go, see them turn and walk out of the room.

- When it feels complete, thank Archangel Michael then gently open your eyes.

- Take notice of any shifts in your body.

As I have grown in my relationship with Niko, this practice has been extremely helpful. I not only use it to cut cords between us, but I also use it to cut cords between my mother and me, my father and me, and the wounded little girl in me to my adult self. All of these relationships affect how I am in my relationship with Niko. My healing work with my parents and my hurt inner child will only benefit my ability to bring my whole self into my marriage. This practice is not to sever my connection with any of these people; I use it to clean up the relationship and bring it into this time and space. I don't want to live from old programming and habits that no longer serve any of us.

Take time now to explore this practice. Which relationships take up the most space in your mind? Start with these and bring them into the present time, by releasing any old cords that no longer serve you, them, or the world.

Drinking in the Joy of You

I am here
Sitting with you
Drinking in the joy
Of you
Present in my life.

Such a simple truth.
Joy bubbles up
When we allow ourselves
To be present to the gift
Of this moment in time.

Sinking into the expanse of deep love,
All we need to do is
Breathe deeply and
Allow this grace to nourish us.

Joy bubbles up
When we allow ourselves
To be present to the gift
Of this moment in time.

Receiving Home, 1995

The Alchemy of Marriage: Receiving Home

NIKO AND I WERE MARRIED IN July of 1995, just twenty-six months after I asked the question in my journal, "Niko, are you who I think you are?" For our gospel reading, we chose the story of Peter trying to walk on water. This is not a common story chosen for weddings, but for me, it felt perfect. Marriage, living intimately with another in a loving way, felt as terrifying and unfamiliar as walking on water. I knew that there would be times when I, like Peter, would succumb to fear and I would begin to sink. It was only with the support and guidance of Spirit that I would be able to navigate this new world.

As I expected, adapting to marriage with Niko was very hard. It felt like another Calcutta experience. Everything felt foreign to me: I slept in a bed snuggled next to Niko; there was no longer a butcher knife under my pillow. We sat at the dinner table, ate delicious dinners, and shared the stories of our day. There was no television in sight to distract us. As I walked into the house, I was greeted by Niko's bright, shining eyes and his joyful "Hello." My need to quickly assess a room to see if it was safe was no longer relevant.

An internal pull to sink into this safe home and the familiar pattern of escaping home were at war within me. The hypervigilance that I had lived for so long felt familiar and comforting. This new experience of home felt vulnerable. It was all I had ever hoped for and yet it was overwhelming. I found myself resisting the open and genuine love Niko offered.

This was so confusing to me. How could I resist the dream that was right there waiting to be embraced? Why did I allow fear to overtake me rather than joy and gratitude? I came to realize that I had never lived with a married couple. By the time I was born, my parents were in a cycle of separation and reconciliation. By the time I was six, my dad was gone from our home for good. I found myself saying to Niko, "If we had five kids and you left me, I would know how to do that. I do not know how to do this!"

The Disney movies I had watched as a child all ended with the couple riding into the sunset and the words printed on the screen, "They lived happily ever after." This was no happily ever after. This was hard! Rage started to surface in me from places I thought had been healed long ago. Before I was married, I thought I had myself put together, but in those honeymoon months, I felt like a total wreck. Niko's gentle spirit provided a safe space that allowed the feelings I had stuffed down as a child to surface. The more out of control I felt, the more I wondered if this marriage was a terrible mistake.

Two things kept me in my marriage every time I felt like walking away. First was my pride. I had stood in front of four hundred people that I deeply loved and respected and made a vow to love and honor Niko all the days of my life. How could I possibly leave after only three months?

Secondly, and most importantly, each time I was tempted to give up, I would take time in stillness, to breathe, and to check in with my spirit. Without fail, I always received clear direction that Niko and our marriage were just what I needed. In spite of all the overwhelming pain and confusion, I needed to stay. I reminded myself that Niko was not getting drunk, cheating on me, wasting our hard-earned money, putting me down or abusing me.

There was no big issue that brought up my rage; it was a million little things. A part of me knew that the anger had absolutely nothing to do with Niko. It was being felt and expressed because of him, but only because he created a safe container. No matter how angry I got, he did not take it personally. He did not shame me, blame me, or take care of me. He let my anger be mine. I both respected and hated him for that.

Two years into our marriage, I attended a workshop by David Spangler, a self-described "practical mystic" who taught the first two courses I took in my graduate program at Seattle University. David is one of the holiest people I have ever met.

During this workshop, someone asked about the concept of "soul mates." David's reply went something like this: "If there is such a thing as a soul mate, then your soul mate is there for your soul's growth. Therefore, they will take you to your very edges. That is where you need to grow." My whole body relaxed.

The voice of fear that would rear its head and tell me I had made a huge mistake in getting married to Niko was released. I could see clearly, that the pain and confusion were the results of my soul travelling in uncharted territory. I was learning to trust, communicate, and settle into home. As a child and teenager, home was most often a place I wanted to get away from. Now I had a home where Niko's face lit up as I walked in the door and delicious aromas from his culinary creations greeted me. I had a home that felt safe and loving and that allowed my spirit to shine. Relaxing into this new reality would take some time. It was everything I had ever wanted and more than I ever imagined.

My marriage offered the opportunity to be seen, known, and loved as well as to see, know, and truly love another.

Sinking into Love, 2011

Write a New Script

WHEN NIKO AND I WERE PREPARING for marriage, we made it very clear to each other that we were committed till "Death do us part." We were also clear that if either of our individual spirits started to die and could not grow in the container of our marriage, then that would be a death that would cause us to part. This commitment to our spirit, and to the spirit of the other, has been the bedrock of our marriage. It is that commitment to my soul's health and growth that encouraged me to stay when my ego wanted to run.

The image of riding into the sunset in eternal bliss with my knight on a white horse was so strong. What my marriage to Niko offered me was more textured and deeper than this old image. My marriage offered the opportunity to be seen, known, and loved, as well as to see, know, and truly love another. This was more frightening to me than the fantasy romance that the old movies fed me.

Many years ago, I went to an all-day workshop led by Angeles Arrien. Angeles was an internationally recognized cultural anthropologist. During the workshop, she explained that ancient and tribal cultures recognize that we live from our daydreams. These daydreams are continuously playing just below our awareness. Some of our daydreams are positive and some are negative. They are like movies that we play over and over in our minds.

I had a library of old, sad movies of drama and trauma in my head. As my dream of home materialized, the old movies of abandonment, rejection, and failure began to replay. These movies told me that if I relaxed into the comfort of home, I would be blindsided by the hurt that would undoubtedly come. If I let myself love and be loved by Niko, he would leave me or somehow be taken from me, and I would crumble. If Niko really knew me, if he saw who I really was, he would not like what he saw, and he would reject me. The old movie that I was not worthy began to roll and filled me with fear and anxiety. I needed new scripts to replace the old, sad movies that would never serve me or my marriage.

Angeles taught us a simple exercise to help us manage the movies in our minds that negatively affect our lives. This simple exercise helps us stop the catastrophic movies and replace them with movies that bring us more joy and peace. The catastrophic movies that we play in our minds are the "what if" daydreams that fuel our fears and fill our lives with anxiety. As easily as we move from one movie to another on Netflix or Hulu, we can deliberately stop an old, repetitive, catastrophic movie in our mind, and replace it with a more positive and life-giving movie.

When our old negative movies begin to play, we simply stop the movie by saying, "Now that's a story that doesn't need to happen. Now that's a story that doesn't need to happen. Now that's a story that does not need to happen." Then we replace the movie with a positive one, by imagining the best possible outcome as we say, "Now that's a healing story. Now that's a healing story. Now that's a healing story."

When Niko is late coming home from work and anxiety begins to churn in my stomach and chest as I imagine him injured in a horrible accident, I deliberately stop that old movie as I repeat three times, "Now that's a story that doesn't need to happen." I actively change the movie in my mind as I imagine Niko walking into the house. I feel him wrap his arms around me as he tenderly says, "Hello. I'm sorry I am late." I breathe in the scent of him as I cuddle into him. Then the two of us sit down to dinner and share the stories of our day. My breath deepens and my heart feels full as I say three times, "Now that's a healing story."

When my opinion differs from others and I am tempted to stay quiet and to keep myself hidden as the old movie of rejection, ridicule, and condemnation begins to play in my mind, I take a deep breath and say three times, "Now that's a story that doesn't need to happen." Then I imagine myself speaking with clarity and authenticity. I allow others to see who I really am and to hear what I really think. I imagine them listening respectfully, and I enjoy our lively discussion. I feel received and respected even as my ideas are challenged. I am at peace within myself as I say three times, "Now that's a healing story."

When I feel sick and my mind starts to imagine that my stomachache must be cancer or my headache is leading to a stroke, I stop myself by saying, "Now that's a story that doesn't need to happen. Now that's a story that does not need to happen. Now that's a story that does not need to happen." Then I imagine myself at an upcoming event healthy and vibrant with no illness or pain. I imagine myself dancing, laughing, and filled with joy as I repeat, "Now that's a healing story. Now that's a healing story. Now that's a healing story."

This practice quiets my anxiety. It allows me to breathe deeply, to bring myself into the present moment and to expand my focus beyond my fears

Exercise: Now That's a Healing Story

Take time throughout the day to track the stories you are creating that feed your anxiety.

Each time your mind starts to play an old familiar catastrophic story, stop it in its tracks.

Use this process to help you shift from a story of drama and trauma to a story of possibility and joy.

- Be attentive to the recurring stories that you play in your head that feed on your fears.

- Each time your mind starts to go to an old familiar catastrophic story choose to stop it.

- Imagine yourself changing channels as you say, "Now that's a story that doesn't need to happen. Now that's a story that doesn't need to happen. Now that's a story that doesn't need to happen."

- Replace your movie of drama and trauma with a movie of possibility and joy.

- Imagine the very best possible outcome and ground that story into your consciousness by repeating, "Now that's a healing story. Now that's a healing story. Now that's a healing story."

Use this process often to expand your focus beyond your fears.

Breakdown

Sometimes I wonder,
Am I having a nervous breakdown?
Break down,
I am breaking down.
I need to be held
So that I can let go
And crumble.
Crumble,
Fall apart,
Piece by piece,
I fall apart.
As I crumble,
I am aware that
I will not return to what I was.
Something new will emerge
From the fragments of
My breakdown.

You are my precious,
my beloved,
my dear child.
My love surrounds you always.

Oregon Coast, 2008

Becoming Home

WHEN I WAS IN MY EARLY twenties, I heard a speaker on the topic of codependency say, "Your unresolved issues with your father will become your issues with your husband or son. Your unresolved issues with your mother will become your issues with your wife or daughter." This statement became a guiding force in my life. I spent the next twenty years consciously working on healing and resolving my unresolved issues with my parents so that I could create a new paradigm of home.

My community of friends was essential in this shift. I surrounded myself with people who provided a new model of family for me. These women and men were masters in the art of loving. I watched them with wonder and awe and drank in the examples of compassionate, loving partnership and parenting they provided.

Their marriages radiated tenderness and respect for one another. It was obvious that they not only loved each other, but actually liked each other and enjoyed being together. They had challenges and difficulties, yet in the midst of their challenges, their love for one another was apparent. When they started having children, I was astounded by how these qualities poured forth into their parenting. I watched them closely and studied their ways as if I was studying a new species.

Stacy lived in a tiny mother-in-law house next to an old farmhouse in the middle of the city. When she married Joe, he moved into this tiny house with her. Before the wedding, Stacy set out to make room for Joe. She cleared one quarter of the space, in her small closet, for his things. When Joe moved in, she soon realized that there was more of Joe than could fit in the small space she had provided. A guiding question for her marriage became, "How do I make room for Joe, not only in my physical space, but in my heart and my life?" Her wisdom became a beacon for me as I sought to become home for Niko. To tend to my marriage, I needed to make space for him in my home, heart, and life. I needed to release any old mindsets, heal unresolved issues, and throw away the perfect pictures that interfered with the real work of loving and being loved.

When Stacy and Joe's young son began rubbing his eyes or showed any signs of discomfort at a gathering, one of them would gently scoop him up and take him to a quiet room. They sat with him there until he fell asleep, even if this meant that they missed the rest of the get-together. This was a new model for me. I was used to children acting out before their need for rest or quiet was acknowledged. They were sent to their rooms and left there to cry it out on their own as if their exhaustion was an imposition. Stacy and Joe taught me about the importance of tuning in to our child's needs and responding compassionately. This was the way I wanted to respond to my child's needs.

When Sarah told her three-year-old son Micah to stop hitting her or he would need to go into time out, Micah looked right at her and hit her again. Sarah took him to his room and told him that he was in time out for three minutes because he hit her. Then she gently left the room and closed the door. After three minutes, she went back to his room, opened the door and said, "OK, lovey, your time out is over; you can come out now." Micah came out of his room and climbed onto his mom's lap. It was over.

It was all so clean. There was no withholding of love, no shaming, nor any kind of rejection towards him for his behavior. Sarah told Micah to stop. She told him what the consequence would be if he did not stop and then she followed through with the consequence. Once the consequence was completed, it was over. I cannot even begin to explain how revolutionary this was for me. Sarah did not in any way communicate to Micah that he was bad. She was consistent with focusing on the behavior. Her love for him was never withheld. This was the way I wanted to discipline my child.

When Shane's children talked to her, she listened to each of their stories with enthusiasm and respect. She did not talk down to them. Her tone of voice was the same tone she used with everyone else. Her love and delight in them were palpable. During one of our visits, her five-year-old daughter Kelby wanted to lead us all in "a moment of peace." Kelby directed us to sit on the floor in crisscross applesauce, to bend our arms at the elbows, and to put our hands up and open at our sides. Then she instructed us, "Close our eyes. Take some deep breaths…Now, enjoy this moment of peace."

We all followed her instructions as if she was an honored teacher and entered into the experience fully. Shane taught me that children are to be seen, heard, and respected. They are our great teachers. This was the way I wanted to honor my child's spirit.

I drank in every new parenting technique I discovered. I spent as much time as I could with these friends so that their approach to partnering and parenting would become the new normal for me.

Two and a half years into our marriage, Niko and I finally conceived. At the time, it felt like forever. In retrospect, I can see that those years we spent trying to conceive were important. We needed that time to learn how to sink into home, to cut any cords to old mindsets that no longer served us, and to deepen our enjoyment of living together, so that we would have enough internal space to receive a child into our lives.

On Halloween night of 1997, I could hardly believe it when my pregnancy test formed a pink positive sign. Niko's face lit up with joy as he bellowed, "We're pregnant!" and took me in his arms. I stared at the stick in disbelief. Tears rolled down my face as I voiced my fear, "What if the test is faulty? What if it's wrong?" Niko ran to the store and bought two more pregnancy tests. Only when they both came back positive did I allow myself to believe it was true. I curled into Niko's embrace and tenderly expressed my joy. My deep dream had taken root.

Just two weeks after our third wedding anniversary, Sam came into the world. I was thirty-eight years old and had waited my whole life for this moment. We spent the first forty days of Sam's life cocooned in our home, bonding as a family. We limited our visitors, spent time cuddled together, learned to respond to Sam's cues, and drank in our new life together. Just as Niko and I had made a commitment to each other's spirit when we married, now we made a conscious commitment to honor, support, and respect Sam's spirit as well. We dedicated ourselves to doing everything in our power to keep his unique spirit intact.

Legacy Fulfilled

WHEN SAM WAS FOUR YEARS OLD, Niko's dad, Ray, whom we affectionately call Papa, came for a visit. Niko drove to pick up Papa at the airport, while I picked Sam up at preschool. I had afternoon clients, so I took Sam to my office, where Niko and Papa would pick him up. When the two of them arrived, I opened my office door to greet Papa, who walked right past me saying, "Where's my boy? Where's my boy?" He walked into the front room where Sam stood giggling. Papa scooped him up in his arms and gave Sam hugs and kisses and delighted in how much Sam had grown. Only when this ritual was completed did Papa come back to where I was standing. He kissed my cheek as he said, "Well hi, Kim!" as if he had just discovered that I was there.

A few moments later, the three of them left. I stood at my office window and watched them walk hand in hand across the street and into the park. I watched them for many minutes while tears streamed down my face and my heart was full to bursting. My tears turned to quiet weeping as I realized I had succeeded in shifting the paradigm of my childhood. Sam had a home where he knew he was loved, wanted, enjoyed, and treasured. He would not be haunted by a dark male presence in his dreams. This was legacy enough.

I am so glad you are here.
I love journeying with you.

Sam and Me, 2003

Journal for Clarity and Empowerment

As we prepared to welcome Sam into our world, I began to make space in my body, mind, and soul for this new life growing inside me. I ate healthy, organic foods, took my prenatal vitamins, and avoided anything that could be harmful to the baby. I studied books on pregnancy and followed the week-by-week development of the growth of our baby inside me. Niko and I took three—yes, three—different birthing classes. I began writing letters in my journal to the child growing within me. These letters not only allowed me to track my feelings but also to set my intention for who I was becoming as a mother.

I had used writing for many years to help me clarify and set intentions for the life I was creating. Before I bought my house, I wrote down the qualities of my ideal home. When I was ready to find a life partner, I wrote in my journal and clarified the qualities of the person with whom I wanted to build a life. As I prepared for motherhood, I wrote about the qualities I wanted to bring to my mothering.

As soon as I became pregnant, I started my journal to Sam. The entries helped me document all that was happening as Sam grew inside me, and then how he grew in the world after he was born. Journaling became a vehicle for me to clarify and own the qualities that I was dedicated to birthing within myself to become the mother I longed to be. These journal entries strengthened in me my dedication to my becoming.

Just two weeks before Sam's birth I wrote:

Hi Sweet Pea,

I have loved being pregnant with you. I cherish this time feeling you move, kick and stretch, and feeling your hiccups. I am not very anxious about labor, but I am anxious about being a mom. I want to be a good mom and I fear that I won't know how.

Two weeks ago, your Papa came and helped your dad prepare the house for your arrival. I watched them very carefully and was overwhelmed by the love and delight they both obviously feel for one another. I never had that kind of relationship with either of my parents. I pray that you and I can share that kind of delight with each other. I pray that I will affirm your uniqueness, highlight your goodness, and create an environment in which you are confident of my love for you and secure in my belief in you. I pray that we will laugh often and enjoy exploring life together. I pray that you will feel free to be <u>who you are</u> and that I won't get in the way of that.

I love you, little precious one, and I await your arrival with joy!

———————◗◆◖———————

When he was six months old, I wrote,

You, my dear son, by your very presence in my life, have called me to a new challenge in my growth...embracing joy. Since your conception, I have found myself growing more and more fearful. I catch myself creating negative fantasies in my mind, fearing something will happen to you or me or your daddy.

I have come to realize that I have everything I've ever wanted and now the life challenge is to allow myself to enjoy it—really soak it in and enjoy it—rather than spending time in fear that something will happen to it. It is taking great discipline and I am determined to master the lesson to live in the here and now. You are a wonder, Sam. You are so full of joy and it is so easy to make you laugh. People look at you and you smile back at them and I watch in awe as their hearts melt and spirits expand to meet you. I am so glad you are here. I love journeying with you.

Writing these entries was essential to my process of becoming the mother I wanted to be. They allowed me to become crystal clear about my vision for my own becoming, for the home I was creating with Niko and Sam, to claim that vision with clarity and conviction, and to track its unfolding. These writings reminded me, "This is who I am, this is who I am, this is who I am." And they empowered me to bring myself more fully into the world.

Exercise: Claim the Vision of Your Becoming

Do you have a journal? If so, go get it. If not, buy one, make one, or dedicate a spiral notebook to be your journal.

- With your journal, find a comfortable place to sit, where you will not be disturbed.

- Ask yourself, "What am I longing to birth into the world?"

- Take time to write a love letter to the You you long to be.

- Be honest with yourself about your fears or the places you feel stuck.

- Affirm where you are being called to grow.

- Claim your vision for yourself with clarity and conviction.

- When you are finished, put your journal in a place where you will see it often.

- Dedicate yourself to take time each day, or each week, to write in your journal.

Use your journal to help you become clear about your dream for yourself, to set your intentions with clarity and conviction, and to track your unfolding.

Precious Child

Precious Child,
My deepest dream
is that you will know
that my love for you
is deep,
and steady,
and strong.
Though there are many things
you could say or do that
would cause my heart to ache with sadness,
my blood to boil with anger,
or my soul to grieve deeply,
There is nothing, my dear one,
Nothing
you can say
or do
to stop me from
loving you.
You are my precious,
my beloved,
my dear child.
My love surrounds you
always.

When I take a breath and move my focus from my
narrow perspective to take in the broader picture,
then I can find peace and clarity of mind.

Lillehammer, 2010

A More Expansive View

BEFORE BECOMING PARENTS, NIKO AND I were very involved in volunteering in our community. Service was important to both of us. Now that Sam had entered our lives, we believed that it was important that we let go of our volunteer activities and focus on becoming home. We agreed that the greatest service we could offer our community was to raise a healthy child who had a strong foundation of love and a deep sense of belonging. The foundation we provided would allow Sam to step with confidence into the world, to feel safe and at home in the world, and to reach out and have a positive impact on the world.

Home became our top priority. We did not want our busyness in the world to stop us from creating a home that nurtured each of us. We spent the months of my pregnancy completing our commitments. From the time Sam was born until he was out of high school, our volunteer activities were either instigated by Sam or were activities that we could do together as a family.

Time for each other became our greatest gift to each other.

When Sam was six years old, we made glycerin soaps to give as Christmas presents. This was a wonderful project to do with our young son. Glycerin is a clear soap that is easy to melt in the microwave and pour into molds. Sam added essential oils to make our soaps smell good, and he added a little plastic animal or trinket to each soap. We worked on this project many days after school. After we had finally finished making and wrapping over fifty soaps for our family and friends, Sam turned to me and said, "Mom, can we make soaps for my classmates, too?"

"Sam, there are twenty-seven kids in your class!"

"I know," he replied

So out came all of our supplies again and together we made twenty-seven more soaps.

Just ten days later, the big tsunami hit Indonesia. As a family, we gave a monetary donation, but in the midst of the suffering of the Indonesian people, it felt insignificant. I turned to Sam and said, "Sam, what if we made more soap and sold it to raise money for the tsunami clean-up efforts?"

"That would be good," he replied.

So out our supplies came once again. This time we invited other children to join us and they responded. Over four hundred children participated: Every child in Sam's school made three bars of soap; four other schools, a Cub Scout group, and families in two neighborhoods all jumped in to make soap for the Tsunami Soap Project. Together we made over 1800 bars of soap and raised $6,000 to help with tsunami relief.

This was the first of many service activities that were inspired by Sam. In ways that I never would have imagined, limiting our service work to that which we could do together actually expanded our work in the world.

In 2010, we went to Oslo, Norway to participate in the Nobel Peace Prize events. This honor was given to us through the Greater Tacoma Peace Prize for my work in creating and facilitating a peace program at Sam's inner-city public school. The peace program was actually the result of a picture that Sam drew in Sunday School. When his teacher invited him to tell us what the picture was about, he responded, "It's a Disco Party for Peace!" As a family, we thought it was a brilliant idea and organized a Disco Party for Peace to celebrate Niko's fiftieth birthday and Sam's First Communion. Over $15,000 was raised to benefit children affected by war in Iraq, Sudan, and Liberia, and to purchase peace education materials for his school. From the monies earmarked for his school, we created the Bryant Peace Committee at Sam's public K-8 inner-city school, Bryant Montessori.

Our time in Oslo was filled with meetings with prominent people working for peace. One such person was a big bear of a man named Steinar Bryn. Steinar is the senior advisor of the Nansen Center for Peace and Dialogue. He has brought together hundreds of groups in conflict, mostly from the Baltic countries. Steinar invites them to the retreat-like setting of Lillehammer, Norway where over a three-week period he creates a safe space for them to begin to dialogue with one another.

After picking us up at the train station, Steinar took us to the area where the 2004 Olympic ski jump competition took place. There is a building right next to the competition area that was built for the Olympics and is now used as a high school. Students spend part of their day doing classwork and the rest of their day working on their ski jumping skills. As we stood at the bottom of the hill, we watched these students fly through the air on their skis, perfecting their jumps and landings.

Returning to the car, Steinar took us up the mountain so that we could look down at the ski jumps and out over the city of Lillehammer. As we viewed this vast expanse, Steinar asked us if we were hikers, then looked at our boots and with excitement said, "I will meet you at the bottom of the mountain! Take those steps and keep to the right. This is an exercise I do with my groups. I bring the two groups up here and then I have them walk down these steps together. See if you can feel the power of this experience as you, too, walk these steps!"

We began our descent. Amidst snow and ice, we gingerly walked down the very steep, steep, metal steps. I found myself contracting in fear. My hands grasped onto the railing, and my shoulders curled up towards my ears. I stared at my feet and gingerly maneuvered the slippery steps, being careful not to fall. My breathing was constricted and I felt nauseous. Suddenly, I stopped and said to Niko, "I am so frightened; I feel like I might vomit!" As I said this, I looked up to see his face. He encouraged me to stop for a few moments. As I rested, I looked up and out and took in the landscape around me. Below us, I saw again the picturesque city of Lillehammer. Straight ahead, I saw snow-covered mountains as far as the eye could see. It was breathtaking! As I breathed in the beauty, I felt my shoulders drop, my breath deepen, and the nausea and fear dissipate. With this new image in front of me, I felt confident that I could make it down these steps safely. I took another deep breath and started walking down, down, down the steps. I would take a deep breath and look up and out at the beauty around me, then back to what was right in front of me, then out to what was all around me, then back to the narrow focus of my feet, then out taking in the wonder and beauty of it all. At times, fear would overtake me again, my steps would become very small, my breath would quicken, and nausea would flow through me. Then I would remind myself to breathe. Again, I would look out over the beauty around me, and I would feel peace infuse me as the fear and nausea released. I couldn't help but imagine what it would be like to take this trip with people I considered my enemies and to feel their fear and their awe right beside mine.

My narrow focus on my feet and the steps quickly became a metaphor for my own narrow focus during times of growth, conflict, confusion, or stress. My focus can become so small and then fear and anger overtake me. When I take a breath and move my focus from my narrow perspective to take in the greater picture, then, I can find peace and clarity of mind.

This ability to move from my narrow perspective into a more expansive view is especially helpful in the ever-changing challenges of parenting. Shortly after we got the diagnosis that Niko's mom, Jerry, was dying, we talked with four-year-old Sam and told him his Nana was very sick. We didn't talk about her dying around him. Shortly thereafter, there was a two-week period where Sam was very clingy. He needed to be near me at all times and constantly wanted to be touching me or held by me. I found myself at my wit's end one day as I was walking up the steps to our bedrooms and Sam was pulling on the back of my shirt as he followed behind me. I could feel the irritation rising in me, so I stopped, took a deep breath and focused my attention beyond my irritation. When we reached Sam's room, I asked,

"Sam, are you clinging to Mama because you are worried about Nana?"

"Yeah," he said, "I am afraid she is gonna die."

I sat down on his bed and looked into his eyes and asked,

"You're afraid Nana is going to die?"

"Yeah, and I am afraid Papa is going to die too."

"Well Sam, Nana is very sick and she may die. Papa is not sick and so I don't think he's going to die anytime soon. What would it be like if Nana died?"

He replied, "Well Papa would be sad because he'd miss her so, so much."

"Yes, Sam, and Daddy would be sad, too, because Nana is his mommy. We are going to need to be very tender with Papa and Daddy because they will be very sad."

Later that night, Sam asked me to lie down with him when he went to bed. I told him that I would sit with him, but I wouldn't lay with him.

With unusual sassiness, Sam replied, "Mom, either you lay down with me or you're going to have to leave this house, and I'm never going to let you back in."

"Well, Sam, I can either sit with you or go back to my room."

"Sit with me." He said grudgingly.

I sat. When Sam's eyes shut and his breath deepened and it seemed like he was asleep, I tried to sneak out. As I gingerly began to raise myself from the bed, he grabbed onto me and said,

"Don't go, Mama, don't go. Don't ever leave me!"

"Sam are you afraid I'm going to leave you?"

"Yeah, I'm afraid both you and Dad are going to leave me."

"Where would we possibly go?"

"Somewhere far, far away…Like Florida."

"Sam, Mom and Dad might go on vacation sometime to Florida, but we will always come back because we are family. Remember when Mom and Dad went to Prosser to see Nana and Papa, and you stayed back and spent time with Sarah and Steve and the kids?"

Sam's eyes lit up as he exclaimed, "Yeah! And Daddy and I went to Prosser, and you stayed here."

"Sam, even if Mom and Dad go away for a while, we will always come back."

"Yeah, you'd miss me too, too much."

"That's right, Sam, we couldn't possibly stay away. We would miss you too, too much!"

That moment on the stairs, when I was constricted in irritation, I could have easily scolded Sam and told him to stop pulling on my shirt. Instead, I chose to stop and look beyond my feelings. This enabled me to see what I did not see before. It allowed me to understand and respond compassionately to the fears and concerns of my five-year-old son. It allowed grace to guide my parenting.

We couldn't possibly stay away.
We would miss you too much!"

Niko and Sam, 2006

Shift Personas

Each of us wears many hats. Being aware of which hat to wear at which time is not as obvious as I once thought. In the previous story, I needed to know when to be boundary setter and when to be mom, teacher, or guide so that I could effectively help Sam navigate through his anxiety.

Many years ago, at a training with Jean Houston, she had each of us make a list of the many different personas or roles we embody in our lives. I had a list of over thirty different roles. They included: mom, wife, daughter, sister, friend, business owner, massage therapist, truth-teller, healer, priestess, spiritual guide, photographer, author, doula, etc. As I sat with this list, I took time to breathe in the complexity of my Self.

Jean had us choose three of our personas and write them down. I chose photographer, mom, and truth-teller. Then she had us name a skill that we wanted to develop. I chose photography.

Then Jean put on some lively instrumental music. She had us stand up, close our eyes, embody the energy of one of the three personas we had chosen, and begin to act out the skill we wished to develop. She encouraged us to move as if we were doing the skill magnificently and with great mastery.

I closed my eyes, put on the persona "Photographer," and imagined I was in a local park with my camera. I started taking pictures. I moved my body to get the best angle with the best light. I arranged items so that their aesthetic was more pleasing to my eye. I felt confident and accomplished. The photos I imagined in my mind were beautiful.

After five minutes, we completed this exercise. Jean asked us to take a few cleansing breaths and return to the room by opening our eyes. We took a few moments to process the experience and then walked around the room to shake off that personality.

Once again, Jean had us close our eyes and instructed us to take on a second persona from our list of three. This time I chose "Mom." She then instructed us to work on the same skill we wanted to develop, for me that was photography, and to do this skill brilliantly from the second persona. I imagined myself back in the park and began acting out taking pictures of what I saw. I could not believe how different taking photographs felt when I approached it from the persona of "Mom." I discovered flowers, bugs, animals, and people to photograph. I saw and heard myself saying to Sam, "Look, Sam, look! Isn't this beautiful? Isn't this amazing? Look at this color of green! See how this moss is growing on the log?" I felt awe and delight as I shared these wonders with Sam. The photos I saw myself take felt joyful and alive.

For the third round of this exercise, I put on the persona of "Truth-Teller" and back to the park I went with my camera. As I took in the images of the park, tears began to flow. I was overcome by the beauty and the fragility of the flowers, trees, animals, and people I photographed. I was not just capturing their physical form, I was capturing their soul as well. I was changed by the photographs I took as Truth-Teller. They were intimate and profound. They told a story.

This experience forever changed the way I take photos. I no longer try to get the perfect shot. I put on my persona of Truth-Teller and attempt to capture the spirit of the person, place, or event. These photos capture more than just the physicality, they capture the enormous beauty of the soul.

This exercise has been invaluable in my parenting. There were times, when it seemed like the obvious persona to use with Sam was that of disciplinarian or taskmaster. By staying open and looking beyond the obvious, I discovered that when Sam was snarky, becoming a comedian was more effective in helping him shift his energy. When he was melting down and enraged, I became his coach, showing him how to get the energy out of his body more effectively by encouraging him to stomp harder, move bigger, and vocalize louder.

One night at dinner, Sam looked at the many dishes of food on the table and said, "I don't want to eat any of this." The dishes that we had prepared were nothing new. Sam had eaten them many times and always enjoyed them. He had noticed that many of his friends got special meals because they did not like what was served, so he thought he would try that with us. I was tempted to put on the persona of disciplinarian and to tell him that he could eat what we had made or not eat at all. Instead, I put on the persona of teacher and said, "That's OK, Sam. You do not need to eat any of this."

"Can you make me some mac n' cheese, Mom?"

"Oh, no, Sam. You do not have to eat what we made, but you cannot have a special meal."

Then with excitement I said to him, "It's OK if you go to bed hungry tonight. What a great learning that will be for you. Do you know that many children around the world go to bed hungry every night? Some children only get one meal a day and often it is only rice."

"Just rice?!!" he asked in astonishment.

"Yes, Sam, just rice. It is a good experience for us to explore what life is like for others around the world."

There was no energy of shame in the words I spoke to Sam. I had put on the energy of a wise teacher who was excited about this learning he would discover.

Sam chose to eat the rice that was prepared for dinner that night. He awoke in the morning hungry and excited for the breakfast we had prepared.

Exercise: Expand Your Role

Take time now to explore this exercise.

- Get out your journal or a piece of paper.

- Write down every persona that lives in you.

- Study the list you have made and honor the complexity of your Self.

- Now choose three personas you would like to explore and a skill you would like to develop.

- Write them down.

- Turn on some lively instrumental music and begin.

- Stand up, close your eyes and begin to act out doing this skill as the first persona on your list. Really embody that persona and move your body as if you have already mastered the skill you want to develop.

- After 3 to 5 minutes, stop performing the skill, and open your eyes.

- Document your experience in your journal. How did you feel? How did the experience of doing this skill from that particular persona feel? What did you notice?

- When you are finished writing, shake off the persona.

- When you are ready, close your eyes again.

- Take a few deep breaths and put on the second persona.

- Again, imagine yourself doing the same skill with mastery from this new persona.

- Move your body as if you are actually doing the skill.

- After 3 to 5 minutes, stop performing the skill and open your eyes.

- Document the experience in your journal. How did you feel? How did the experience of doing this skill from that particular persona feel? What did you notice? How did doing the skill from this persona feel different from the first persona?

- When you are finished writing, shake off the persona.

- When you are ready, close your eyes.

- Take a few deep breaths and put on the third persona.

- Imagine yourself doing the same skill with mastery from this new persona.

- Move your body as if you are actually doing the skill.

- After 3 to 5 minutes, stop performing the skill and open your eyes.

- Document the experience in your journal. How did you feel? How did the experience of doing this skill from that particular persona feel? What did you notice? How did the doing of the skill feel differently from the first and second personas?

- When you are finished writing, take a few deep breaths and release the persona.

Use this exercise to help you expand your options in tending to your life.

Unearthing Myself

Unearthing Myself.
Finding places that are stuck,
Hardened, Immobile.
Welcoming fluidity.
Moving with my power.
Standing in My Truth.
I Am.

She ran to greet her beloved with her eyes wide open,
ready to received her, just as she was.

Sr. Brian and Sr. Mary Helene, 2006

Unfettered Love

I LOVE VISITING ST. BEN'S, THE college that Father Cody encouraged me to enter over forty years ago. As soon as I see the church dome from Interstate 94, my eyes begin to fill with tears. St. Ben's has consistently called me home to my deepest and most authentic self and invited me to bring her more fully and powerfully into the world. It is my spiritual home. When I walk the paths around campus, I feel my heart soften, then swell, as deep joy and peace become my companions.

The soul of St. Ben's is the monastery. I respectfully refer to the women who live there as a group of "kick-ass nuns." Sr. Mary Helene and Sr. Brian were my two favorites. When I was a student, Sr. Mary Helene was the resident staff person on my freshman dorm floor. Sister Brian's office was strategically placed so that we had to walk by it to get to our dorm rooms. These women embodied the Benedictine values of hospitality and relationship with their loving presence, their blind eye to our antics, and a deep belief in each of us.

After I graduated, I especially loved visiting campus when Sr. Mary Helene was the director of the Monastery's House of Hospitality. She always welcomed me as a daughter. When I went out for a walk, I often came back to find hot cookies or a bowl of popcorn next to my bed. Sr. Mary Helene kept herself available in the library, invited me to join her for prayer or a meal, yet she never intruded on my quiet space. In her presence, I felt loved, seen, nurtured, respected, and enjoyed.

On a visit to St. Ben's in 2002, I spent time visiting with Sr. Mary Helene over a cup of tea. I asked her questions about her life and was surprised by how grateful she felt for the life she had lived. She shared that she had been engaged to a wonderful young man and ended her engagement to join the monastery. I asked her if she ever regretted her decision. Her response was a clear "No" followed by the exclamation, "Who am I to have lived such a life!" Sr. Mary Helene's was just a couple of years younger than my mom, and I could not help but compare my mom's regrets and Sr. Mary Helene's gratitude. I made a clear decision that day that I would live my life in such a way that joy, gratitude, and grace would grow more vivid with each passing year.

On that same visit, I went for a walk with Sr. Brian, and she shared with me that she had just been diagnosed with Alzheimer's. I was honored and surprised by her transparency and willingness to share this with me. I was moved by her acceptance of the path ahead. Sr. Brian showed me that we can be vulnerable and strong at the same time, we can share our heartaches and difficulties without the drama of victimhood, and we can allow others to walk the path with us.

In 2006, I went back to St. Ben's to visit Sr. Mary Helene and Sr. Brian. Sr. Brian's Alzheimer's had progressed and she was living in a Benedictine Care facility in St. Cloud. Once again, Sr. Mary Helene welcomed me as a daughter and invited me to join the sisters at a special Memorial Day lunch. She bubbled with excitement as she told me that Sr. Brian was coming home for the meal.

As we gathered for lunch, I was seated at a table with Sr. Mary Helene and four other sisters. A sixth chair waited for Sr. Brian. As we visited, Sr. Mary Helene watched with anticipation for Sr. Brian's arrival. As soon as she saw the van drive up, Sr. Mary Helene jumped out of her seat and ran to greet her friend. Sr. Mary Helene was eighty-two years old, and she literally ran to welcome Sr. Brian home. What was even more poignant for me, was that Sr. Brian's spirit was rarely visible. Her once lively face now held a blank stare. During our meal, for just a moment, something shifted and the twinkle came back into her eyes. She was home with us and then, just as quickly, she was gone again.

I was deeply moved by that greeting. I was moved that Sr. Mary Helene, who was visiting Sr. Brian two or three times a week, still leapt with joy and ran to greet her friend. She did not expect anything in return. She ran to greet her beloved with her eyes wide open, ready to receive Sr. Brian just as she was. As I witnessed Sr. Mary Helene greet Sr. Brian, all I could think was, "That is the kind of friend, mother, and wife I want to be."

I want to embrace my beloveds with that same unfettered and unconditional love. For the first years of my marriage, when I received that kind of greeting from Niko, I could only give "a deer in the headlights" stare in return. Slowly, I learned how to lean in and receive it. Sam broke through my inhibitions. It was easy to receive his joy and love and return it full-heartedly. How can anyone resist the love of a child? I experience a similar embrace from a handful of close friends. I continue to be a work in progress as I inch my way towards my free expression of joy and love.

Sr. Mary Helene is my guide. Her open-hearted and exuberant greeting of Sr. Brian is imprinted in my memory. In her, I see the freedom, love, and joy I seek to embody and bring to my world. This is my intention. This is the ongoing work of my life. This is my prayer.

"You are just where you need to be.
Take your time.
Relax.
You can do this.
You, my love, are enough.
You are more than enough!

Blessed by My Circle of Women the Week Before I Wed
June, 1993

Exercise: Meet Your Whole Self/Holy Self

The beauty of Sr. Mary Helene's embrace of Sr. Brian embodied for me the soul of relationship. It reminds me to run with my heart and my arms wide open to greet each day, each experience, and each season of life. I am reminded to embrace my beloveds wholeheartedly and respond to the beloved alive in each person I encounter, no matter their race, sexuality, nationality, or gender. Each and every person is worthy of this kind of divine presence. Perhaps, most importantly, it calls me to embrace the beloved within myself—to welcome my spirit, to listen to her whisperings, and to act on my soul's deep yearnings.

Jean Houston led me through the following exercise that has been especially helpful in embracing the beloved within myself. For this exercise, I use the image of a woman and the pronoun she. If a different images and/ or pronoun suits you better, please use it.

- Put on some gentle instrumental music.

- Stand up where you have plenty of room.

- Close your eyes.

- Take a few deep breaths.

- With your palms facing forward, bend your elbows, bringing your forearms up in front of you until your forearms are at waist height.

- Keeping your hands open, take a few more deep breaths.

- Now imagine a woman coming towards you.

- She is the woman you would be if you had a thousand lifetimes to perfect this human experiment that is your life.

- As she reaches you, she stands in front of you and gently rests her palms on yours and looks into your eyes as you look into hers.

- What do you see in her eyes?

- What do you feel?

- What is her message for you?

- When it feels complete, feel her remove her hands. Take a few cleansing breaths.

- Now slowly turn your body around so that you are now standing where she was standing.

- Turn your palms downs and see your current self standing before you.

- Put your palms gently against the open palms before you.

- Look into the eyes of your current self.

- What do you want to communicate to your current self before you?

- Allow your eyes, your presence, and your words to communicate everything you want her to know.

- Now remove your hands from hers.

- Close your eyes again.

- And as you take a few more deep breaths, gently turn yourself around.

- When you are ready, gently open your eyes and come back to this time and place.

- When you are finished, record what you experienced in your journal.

This exercise has been transformative. When I begin to doubt myself and question whether I am doing the right thing or whether I am enough, I take ten minutes to do this exercise. When I stand in the place of my whole Self and put my hands on the hands of my current self, with all her doubts and fears, I feel my whole Self meet her with the same joy and love that Sr. Mary Helene met Sr. Brian. I hear her whisper to me with clarity and love, "You are just where you need to be. Take your time. Relax. You can do this. You, my love, are enough. You are more than enough!" I feel my heart swell and my whole body relax. All my doubts disappear as I am infused with the love and acceptance of my whole and holy Self.

The New Becoming

The old paradigm is dying.
The new paradigm emerges.
Those committed to the old hold on,
Fearful of what is to come.

We are the doulas of the new becoming.
We must radiate the path with our brilliance.
We can no longer muzzle our truth,
Or curl in, protected by our fear.

We must remove our cloak of protection,
Put on our cape of courage,
And stand as priestess, shaman, guide
And assist in the birth
Of the New Becoming.

In Gratitude

I AM DEEPLY GRATEFUL TO ALL who have supported and guided me in my quest to bring my spirit more fully into the world. There are too many of you to list here, but I do want to mention a few of you by name.

To my teachers and mentors: Fr. Nicholas Cody, Terrill Gibson, Betsy Beckman, Jean Houston, David Spangler, Nancy Rebecca, Daphne Michaels, Mary Ellen Floyd, and Bill and Judy Kelly: Your work has expanded my mind and spirit and has called me to evolve beyond my comfort zone. Thank you.

To my book doulas: Bill Kelly, Judy Kelly, and Diane Lachel, your commitment to walking this journey with me and consistently calling me forward to be more clear, honest, and courageous has fueled the fire of this project.

Cathy Donovan, thank you for faithfully standing witness to my unfolding for over forty years. You are a sister of my heart. Thank you for holding my hand and receiving every phone call and answering every question with expertise, creativity, wisdom, and love. I am forever grateful.

To my design and production team: Amy Marc, thank you for your creativity and exquisite use of color and space. You have created a cover that beautifully reflects the message of this book. Susan Lawler, thank you for reading and rereading my manuscript and for capturing and correcting every grammatical error. Your keen eye for detail is a pure gift. You are a proofreader extraorinaire! And to my publishing sherpa, Eva Long, thank you for your gentle encouragement, wise counsel, and commitment to the spirit of this project. Your support and input throughout the process of bringing *Spirit Embraced* into the world has been invaluable.

To my beloveds: Hlony Mary Mokete, thank you for honoring me as a mentor, mother, and wise woman. Thank you for your enthusiasm for *Spirit Embraced* and for encouraging me to get it finished and to bring it into the world. You are my muse.

Sam, thank you for bringing me back to play and relaxation. Thank you for still cuddling on the couch to watch a movie, for making time for family fun and for making me laugh until I cry. Being your mom is the great adventure of my life.

And Niko, thank you for loving me, seeing me and believing in me. Thank you for nurturing my body, mind, and spirit, and for keeping me watered and fed throughout this process. You are my biggest cheerleader, my beloved, my sweet home. I love you so.

KIM COLELLA

KIM COLELLA CALLS HERSELF A SPIRIT Doula. Her mission is to assist women in birthing their spirits into the world and to reclaim the sacred dimension of their own physical being. Kim founded Body Sacred, her healing practice in Tacoma, Washington in 1991.

Kim has followed her spirit's urging to embrace life in all its complexity. She ministered to both the elderly and teens as a Jesuit Volunteer; traveled to Calcutta to meet and experience the work of Mother Theresa; joined a delegation of women to witness the AIDS pandemic in South Africa; designed and implemented a Peace Program for her son's inner-city public school, assisted over 25 women in giving birth, helped others prepare for their deaths and co-authored *Lasting Gifts: Living with Intention and Dying in Peace.* Such experiences have fostered in her a deep awe and respect for each phase of life.

Kim is a Spirit Doula, Restorative Touch™ practitioner, licensed massage therapist, photographer, author, and philanthropist. Her purpose is to be an evocator of the Sacred and to help others celebrate its magnificence in themselves, their relationships, and their world.

Kim is a graduate of the College of St. Benedict and holds a Master of Arts in pastoral studies with an emphasis in spirituality from Seattle University. She is the recipient of the 2016 Service Award and the 1992 Decade Award from the College of St. Benedict, the 2013 Alumni of Distinction Award from Hill- Murray High School and is the 2010 Laureate of the Greater Tacoma Peace Prize.

She lives with her husband Niko and son, Sam, in Tacoma, Washington. To learn more about Kim and her work, visit spiritdoula.com.

CPSIA information can be obtained
at www.ICGtesting.com
Printed in the USA
FSHW021726180619
59174FS

9 781733 012409